PARENTING
Bright Kids
Who *Struggle*
in *School*

PARENTING
Bright Kids
Who *Struggle*
in *School*

A Strength-Based Approach to Helping
Your Child Thrive and Succeed

Dewey Rosetti

PRUFROCK PRESS INC.
WACO, TEXAS

Library of Congress information
on file with the publisher.

Copyright ©2020, Prufrock Press Inc.

Edited by Stephanie McCauley

Cover and layout design by Allegra Denbo

ISBN-13: 978-1-64632-033-2

Printed in the United States of America.

At the time of this book's publication, all facts and figures cited are the most current available. All telephone numbers, addresses, and website URLs are accurate and active. All publications, organizations, websites, and other resources exist as described in the book, and all have been verified. The author and Prufrock Press Inc. make no warranty or guarantee concerning the information and materials given out by organizations or content found at websites, and we are not responsible for any changes that occur after this book's publication. If you find an error, please contact Prufrock Press Inc.

 Prufrock Press Inc.
P.O. Box 8813
Waco, TX 76714-8813
Phone: (800) 998-2208
Fax: (800) 240-0333
http://www.prufrock.com

Dedication

To my wonderful daughters and my sainted husband, who
encouraged me to finish what I started. We did it!

Table of Contents

Acknowledgments ix

Foreword
by Todd Rose xi

Introduction
A Child's Cry for Help 1

Part I: From Surviving to Thriving

Chapter 1   Not Like the Others 11
Chapter 2   Turning the Tide 23

Part II: Changing the Mindset

Chapter 3   Mindset Is Key 35
Chapter 4   The Deceptive Language of Disability 43

Part III: A New Way of Thinking

Chapter 5   From High School Dropout to Harvard Scientist 61
Chapter 6   Jaggedness: *The Norm, Not the Exception* 69
Chapter 7   Context: *The Key to Unlocking Talent* 77
Chapter 8   Pathways: *Always More Than One* 85

Part IV: The Way Ahead

Chapter 9   Success Stories 93
Chapter 10   Case Studies 103
Chapter 11   The Coming Revolution 119

Recommended Resources 129

References 137

Appendix A   Understanding the Psych-Ed Report 141

Appendix B   Sample Psych-Ed Report 145

About the Author 177

Acknowledgments

Thank you to the following people:

My sister Maureen Bruce, who attended all of those early Parents Education Network (PEN) events and presented me with a mock-up book prototype in 2005, my name on the cover as the author. Its inspiration became a burden of guilt as the years ticked by with no published title. Finally, I can say thank you.

My sister, Kathleen Sweazey, who generously supported me with her time, ideas, and donations from that first meeting in 2002.

Todd Rose, a friend and mentor, and most of all a teacher who has shared most generously his time and thinking to help me create a viable tool for parents. Without him, this book would not exist.

James Hider, a journalist who enthusiastically took what I had written and made it into a marketable draft while also serving as chief encourager and cheerleader.

Megan Malone, for her original writing.

Robin Schader, a colleague who introduced me to Prufrock Press and my editor, Stephanie McCauley.

All of the wonderful people I have met through PEN, starting with Rosalie Whitlock, our original advisor, nonstop cheerleader, and now preserver of EdRev through Children's Health Council. PEN Board members and PEN advisors, you know who you are, who generously gave your time, advice, experience, and credibility to our original parent group as we searched for ways to support PEN members. PEN's student group SAFE, whose members spoke respectfully and eloquently about their educational experiences. The parents and kids who agreed to be in case studies.

Natalie O'Byrne, my mentor who has brought me along over 25 years from a fixed to a growth mindset in so many aspects of my life.

Foreword

When parents hear from a teacher that their child is struggling in the classroom, their first thought is usually, "What's wrong?" They can feel as though their world has been shaken because the assumption is that there must be something wrong with their child.

If this happens to you, you will likely find that your whole concept of parenting is suddenly under fire: Your child may be labeled as being "different" from other kids, and you will find yourself in an unfamiliar new world. It is not unusual to feel paralyzed by the experience as you struggle to understand your child's needs and potential, and even where your child will fit in school, future employment, and society.

Parenting Bright Kids Who Struggle in School is designed to serve as the first port of call to this unfamiliar landscape, and Dewey Rosetti is your ideal guide. She knows what you are going through because she experienced it herself. With her own daughter failing at school, Dewey spent years educating herself about the limits of one-size-fits-all education in order to ensure that her daughter received the schooling she deserved. But Dewey didn't stop there; wanting to share her hard-won knowledge, she launched a nonprofit to help parents and teachers understand what bright and often-misunderstood kids need to thrive. It was in this context that we came to know each other.

My own work is in a field called the "Science of Individuality." This science rejects the idea of an average person and focuses on understanding the uniqueness of individuals. What we have found from this science is truly remarkable: We know that individuality is the rule, not the exception, that all people differ in meaningful ways in terms of learning and development, and that forcing a cookie-cutter approach, whether in medicine or education, both harms individuals and is counterproductive for society. The insights from this science made possible efforts to personalize everything from medicine to education.

Even though many people have benefited from the insights of the Science of Individuality, most parents probably haven't heard of it. This is, in part, because there has not been a credible effort to translate its vital lessons into actionable insights for parents.

That is where Dewey steps in. After 25 years of self-education about the field of learning sciences and the various ways that different children approach learning, her perspective evolved from blaming the "square peg" child to identifying the serious faults in our outdated education system with its one-size-fits-all approach. She has taken the lessons of individuality, as well as important works of leading educators, psychologists, and neuroscientists, and communicated them in an accessible way for stressed parents to understand how they can start helping their child right now.

Dewey's story of her own experience battling the standardized education system shows that it is possible for parents to move beyond their initial paralysis and discover a whole new way of supporting their child, one that builds upon their child's strengths and mitigates weaknesses. This is a method that can apply to *any* child, no matter their starting point. You just have to look at the success stories featured in the latter chapters of this book to understand how a wide range of kids who might otherwise have been written off by an overburdened and underfunded educational system can be nurtured into successful young adults.

I am in awe of Dewey's journey and her contributions: from a passionate parent focused on solving the problems facing her little girl, to a social entrepreneur who helped thousands of kids and parents in her state, to a national leader bringing these ideas to *all* parents to help them support *all* children in realizing their full potential regardless of who they are or where they are starting their journey. She is nothing less than inspiring, and I cannot think of a more trustworthy person to take worried parents by the hand and lead them on this new path.

This book will not be the last book parents will read in searching for answers, but it should be the first one they reach for.

—Todd Rose, Harvard Graduate School of Education

Introduction

A Child's Cry for Help

In March of my daughter's third-grade year, I received a phone call from her school principal. I had gotten used to such phone calls by then and answered with some trepidation. Sensing my nervousness, Ms. K, the lower school head, hurried to reassure me. "Melissa is okay," she said, "but we need to talk to you right away."

As soon as I walked into my daughter's elementary school, I could tell something was wrong. Ms. K always tried to maintain a friendly demeanor, but she had a telltale flush on her neck that betrayed her real mood. Today, it was flashing red like a danger signal and rapidly spreading to her cheeks. I felt queasy as soon as I saw her.

"Ms. K, is everything okay? Are you alright?" I asked. It has always been my instinct to try to calm people down and reassure them, even though, on this occasion, it was I who needed reassurance.

Instead of motioning me toward her office as she usually did, Ms. K ushered me into a very small, windowless room—a kind of converted closet—that I had never seen before. As I looked in, I saw my daughter's teacher, Ms. P, her gray-white face in stark contrast to Ms. K's flushed complexion. Her eyes were wide open with—what? Alarm . . . anger? Her expression was unreadable in my own rising anxiety.

Ms. P was holding something in her lap that looked like a piece of paper. She and Ms. K both motioned to me to sit down on one of the two folding chairs jammed in the tiny room. Ms. P and I were knee to knee; Ms. K remained standing. She nodded to Ms. P to show me what she was gripping tightly in her lap.

As the teacher extended the paper with shaking hands, she turned it over so I could see what was drawn on it. I saw an unsophisticated picture of a little girl with bright yellow hair and blue eyes, dressed in a green plaid jumper reminiscent of the school uniform. The child was facing forward, toward the viewer, and next to her was a roughly sketched building: the school, identified by its initials.

The little girl had a lit match in her cartoon-like hand, and the bright orange flame was touching the building.

Now I could understand the two teachers' alarm, even their fear. To them, the drawing probably looked like a flashing warning signal. But all I could think of was that my little girl, still only in third grade, had already gotten to the point where she had decided to draw this horrific image of how she felt about school.

My daughter Melissa was, like me, a people pleaser. She had extra sensors for people's disapproval. She certainly knew when she drew this picture that it would not be met with approval or praise. I felt a deep sadness for Melissa because she hated this school so much that she had to risk such crushing disapproval in order to make her pain known. I felt disappointed that I had let things go this far without protecting her. Every day had been a battle to conform to a place where she just did not—and could not—fit in. I quietly took the drawing from the teacher and stared at it more closely, imagining my little girl shouting at me in a fit of frustration, "Get me out of here!"

I looked around at this little secret room and saw it as a place of shame—shame for my daughter, drawing a picture of herself doing something as awful as burning down the school, and shame for myself, that I had not recognized how much my child was suffering.

I knew something had to change.

How Did We Get Here?

My husband and I had not specifically selected the all-girls school that Melissa now wished so desperately to escape. It was simply the school we had sent our older daughter to. I felt that if it had worked for her, it would work for our younger one, too. I was very mistaken.

There had been signs that Melissa might face hurdles ahead, but they were far from conclusive, and besides, we were ill-equipped at the time to recognize them. We had been told when she was accepted into kindergarten that she might have some language issues, a fact picked up on by the admissions committee during the original interview sessions. The committee members wrote us a letter before school had even started, saying that they would be watching out for any language problems so they could quickly intervene with special help.

It wasn't that the school personnel didn't want to help Melissa—they actually provided hundreds of hours of extra tutoring over the years—but they simply did not know how to teach her to read. Conventional methods did not work, and after 4 years of relying on the school, she had fallen so far behind that she became increasingly frustrated and angry. Once confident, compliant, and wanting to please, she became negative and totally unsure of herself. Her personality morphed into an oppositional one.

I wondered for years after that why I hadn't taken action earlier to move Melissa from that school. Now, some 20 years later, I can clearly state the reason: I didn't know what to do if the school itself couldn't help her. I am ashamed to say I was willing to think that she might not be smart enough to be at that school. In other words, I thought it was my daughter's fault that she wasn't learning, and probably my fault for choosing the wrong school for her. I naively thought that schools and teachers were the experts in teaching *all* kids—and that, it turns out, is not true. In my experience with teachers from all types of schools, 99% of educators are passionate about helping their students learn. But unfortunately, teacher education—especially on the subject of different types of learning styles—is woefully behind the science.

The fact that many children are unable to learn according to the way their particular schools teach them is becoming more and more evident to parents and teachers. Unfortunately, schools are lagging well behind the science in adopting teaching practices that work for different types of thinkers. In fact, it is estimated that at least one in five students in the

U.S. have a learning difference (National Center for Learning Disabilities [NCLD], 2017). That figure is likely much higher, given the reluctance of many schools to identify and acknowledge the problem in order to avoid offering the services needed, as well as the reluctance of some parents to have their children tested due to the stigma attached to a learning disability label.

In the past 10 years, neuroscience has shed light on the unique variability of the individual brain, but it will be years before appropriate teaching methods for these different brain types will catch up. In the meantime, if your child is struggling with learning, it may be that their school is not a good fit for the type of brain they have, and therefore for their learning needs. In this case, it is up to you, as the parent, to fill in the gaps between what the school can teach them and how their brain needs to learn. This may sound, at first, like a daunting prospect. But the primary aim of this book is to guide you through this process.

Teachers may have told you where your child's shortfalls lie. Maybe your child doesn't seem engaged, isn't trying hard enough, and causes disruption in class. Maybe the problem is more specific, like reading at a level below classmates, underperforming in math, or writing illegibly. Or maybe your child isn't socially adept, seems to lack necessary confidence, or doesn't have any friends. Maybe your child is telling you themselves that they are dumb, stupid, or hate themselves.

If any of this is happening, no matter how old your child is, you need to get more information about the situation as soon as you can. Your child is likely suffering from a poor fit between their learning profile and what the school deems ideal. This means that the school's teachers are teaching to a particular audience—of which your child is not a member. Your child then feels like a misfit, an outsider. This isolation may cause your child to act out and behave in a way that shows, rather than tells, you how unhappy they are. This happened in the case of my daughter. It took years before I cracked the code on how to help her succeed both in school and later in life.

Don't Panic! But Don't Delay

When someone tells you that something isn't right about your child, a part of you dies. Call it the idea of your "perfect" child—that image of your kid's future trajectory, replete with all of the fantasies of a fulfilling life and the effortless accolades they will enjoy. That all seems to vanish in a puff of smoke. How will your child survive school, where test scores and grades are all-defining? How will your child survive college and a career, when tasks that seem easy for others cause your child to break down and stumble?

But all is not lost. You've seen your child excel in certain tasks and in certain contexts. You know that your child has intelligence and capabilities. A learning disability diagnosis is not a death sentence—far from it. It can be an opportunity to dig deep into your child's mind, explore how they learn as an individual, understand their strengths and weaknesses, and determine which pathways to learning will best set them up for success. It is an opportunity to have an even deeper relationship with your child.

When it became clear that my daughter wasn't going to learn to read in the usual way—automatically, the way I had learned to read—I was thrown off. I felt helpless and alone, flummoxed as I tried to figure out the best ways to help her. I didn't know how to teach a child to read, so who did? I found out that there were, in fact, people who addressed such problems, but they weren't working at the school she was attending.

In addition, I quickly realized I had a great deal of parenting work to do. I had to help my daughter navigate schools that were ill-equipped to maximize her strengths, and to help her establish a sense of accomplishment and self-esteem in a system where she was constantly failing.

In short, I had to educate myself, along with educating my little girl.

The Road Less Traveled

Although I didn't realize it at the time, I was about to embark on a road traveled by millions of American parents every year. Experts say that one in five American kids experience some kind of learning difficulty (NCLD, 2017), but that statistic does not describe the sheer range of neurodiversity out there, from the often-misunderstood label of dyslexia, to Attention Deficit/Hyperactivity Disorder (ADHD), to processing issues and autism spectrum disorders (ASD).

Each of these learning difficulty labels refers to a part of the brain that isn't performing in an "average" way. The labels can be useful in helping doctors, teachers, and therapists pinpoint where a child's struggles originate. However, as scientists and researchers learn more about the brain and how it operates, these diagnostic boundaries are anything but clear. Studies from institutions like Harvard University (Rose, 2016), as well as my personal communications with cofounders of the University of California, San Francisco Dyslexia Center (S. Carnevale & D. Evans, 2018), indicate that each individual's neural profile is unique. Most researchers admit that labeling people according to brain differences is absurdly limiting—like labeling people for having different fingerprints.

Few parents look at their infants and worry about learning challenges, sensory processing issues, or ADHD. With babies, parents seek signs of intellectual awakening (e.g., "Look, she's mimicking me! She's looking where I point!"). As babies grow into toddlers, parents giddily check off developmental milestones: first wobbly steps, first mangled sentences, sleep training, potty training, etc.

Sometimes, developmental issues become clear early on, but more often, parents think their children are utterly and completely normal—until they go off to school. Then parents learn to see through another lens, one focused on a school's narrow definition of intelligence, academic achievement, and success, which is often simply measured by comparison with children's peers. If a child doesn't easily conform with that mold, the preschool and early elementary years may mark the beginning of a struggle that can last for decades.

Perfection, Lost

When you learn that your child is different from the others and is suddenly facing a future littered with learning challenges, the experience is akin to that of loss. Experiencing the loss of the idea of a "perfect" child can cause pain and paralysis—it's so hard to know what to do next that many parents either get sucked into a downward spiral of grief or freeze up and take no action at all.

In retrospect, I allowed my daughter to remain in a school where she wasn't able to learn for too long, and she paid the price for it, both in a loss of self-esteem and a daunting anxiety that interfered with her learning and social interactions. In that sense, the problem came down to me. The lack of guidance on different strategies for handling my daughter's obvious inability to learn to read, after 4 years of the same kind of remediation by her school, came as a surprise to me back then in the 1990s. But so many parents today still face the same issue.

After 25 years of talking to schools and teachers, I am certain that the problem is not the attitude of the teacher in most cases, but rather the lack of good information and education about how to identify and deal with different learners in the classroom. There is little up-to-date information about learning and the brain in graduate schools of education. I know my daughter's school didn't alert me earlier because the teachers were not really aware of the signs of dyslexia and other learning differences. Even if they had been, back then it was thought that children could not be accurately tested for challenges until the second or third grade. Thankfully, this is no longer the case.

Problem solving for Melissa changed my worldview in ways I couldn't have imagined. It inspired me to cofound an organization for parents (Parents Education Network, or PEN) that started in my living room and grew to include thousands of members across four states, and then became part of much larger, nationwide groups. What started out as a simple impulse to help my daughter survive evolved into a drive to help all children—indeed, all *people*—thrive in their educational environments, careers, and interpersonal relationships. Now that my daughter is a successful adult—a college grad and real estate entrepreneur—I feel comfortable sharing her story. I also want to share stories of success that I witnessed working with scores of other families through the years.

Through the work of forward-thinking scientists and researchers, a growing movement supports the fact that learning "differently" is, in fact, the norm. Each person has a different profile of strengths and weaknesses, as unique as a fingerprint. Putting each individual child in charge of their own personal learning profile, so that they can choose the right direction for their future, should be the goal of every parent—and school.

In my case, I had to dismantle a whole pyramid of wrongheaded assumptions before I could recognize and embrace the individual talents of my child. I had been conditioned to assume that there was just one specific, one-dimensional kind of intelligence. By thinking that talent and intelligence were fixed traits that a person either does or doesn't have, I severely limited my chances of understanding my child's individual strengths and weaknesses and helping her to ultimately follow her own path.

In the past decade, the field of neuroscience has made stunning progress in the understanding of how kids' brains work and how children learn individually. Without doubt, we are on the verge of an educational revolution that will challenge the school system and reshape the learning experience of every child. Help is on the way. But your child's school is probably not there yet, and you may find yourself struggling in the new land of learning differences, with its own language and ways.

This book will act as your guide, helping you navigate this new environment and its confusing language. I will take you through my own journey, from parenting a child with different learning needs, to cofounding a parents' network, to my exposure to new groundbreaking ideas about intelligence, talent, success, and learning. Mine is a journey of discovery, above all, of how to nurture self-esteem and resilience. These ideas have changed my life, and I have no doubt that they will soon be changing the wider culture, too.

My hope is to present you with the information you need to take a deep breath and step back from the panic you might be feeling when you first learn that your child is one of the 20% who don't learn in the way that their school expects them to (NCLD, 2017). Even if your child does learn in expected ways, the parenting advice contained in these pages will help any parent encourage their child to develop their strengths and minimize their weaknesses.

Using the science of a growing group of experts from across a variety of related fields, I will show that the new model of learning—growth mindset, strength-based and positive thinking, and long-view parenting—is the best way to help your child understand their unique pathway to success and fulfillment in life.

The time to start your parenting plan is right now.

Part I
From Surviving to Thriving

CHAPTER 1

Not Like the Others

September 10, 1996, seemed like any other Tuesday night at first. Melissa was 6 years old, and I was in the upstairs bathroom trying to wrangle her into the tub. Most nights, it was a struggle to get this little one bathed and in bed at a reasonable hour; she was a spirited, energetic kid. I had hoped that starting kindergarten might wear her out a bit, but we were 5 days into the school year, and she showed no signs of slowing down. That night she futzed around outside the tub, talking to her Barbies and doing anything she could to delay the inevitable.

"Come on, honey. Let's go," I called out. "You can bring the Barbies into the bath with you. Let's get this done."

I steeled myself for the usual protests, but instead, she burst into tears and yelled, "How can you be so *mean* to your child?" Hiccup. "A child who has had such a terrible day?"

I started to smile at first; Melissa could be a bit of a kidder at times. But then she literally dropped to a heap on the floor. Through her hiccups and sobs—the kind that make you think your kid may stop breathing at any minute—she blurted out, "The teacher asked us all to sound out a word today and I had no idea what she meant. And *all* of the other girls knew how to do it. I don't know what that means: 'sound it out.'"

I sank down on the floor and faced her squarely, so she would know she had my attention. By nature, Melissa was a willful child, already very competitive, always racing ahead of anyone who tried to walk beside her. Since the age of 2, she had been the personification of "I can do it myself!" In keeping with her independence, she didn't like to be hugged much either, even by me. Her willingness to come unglued raised a big red flag.

"Honey, can you remember what the word was?" I asked.

"It was 'cat.'"

I showed her: "First you say 'ccc' for 'C' and then 'aaa' for 'A' and then 'ttt' for 'T.' Cat is spelled C-A-T." I looked at her wonderfully expressive face, knitted brows, and welling eyes.

"Yes, that's what they said. But I still don't know what that means," she repeated.

"Well, honey, it's only the second week of school. I'm sure the teacher didn't expect everyone in the class to understand sounding it out right away."

This idea didn't calm her down at all: "No, mommy, everyone really *did* know how to do it, except me."

With that, I pulled her up and moved her toward the tub, which I now saw as a calming activity more than a chore. The bath worked as a distraction. She stopped crying and calmed down enough to let me bathe her and help her get into her pajamas. She was definitely still sad but no longer sobbing, and there was no more talk of her day at school.

When I had finally gotten my red-eyed and splotchy little one in bed, my mind flitted briefly back to the letter we had gotten from the school right after Melissa was admitted. The testing that every child went through during the application process did, in fact, show that Melissa might have some trouble with words and letters. But the school had accepted her anyway, probably because our older daughter was now a fifth grader there and our family loved the school.

Warning Signs

As I dropped Melissa off at school the next morning, I thought about how much I loved the atmosphere of the place—so different from the Catholic schools I'd attended as a girl, where there was always the nagging thought that I might be doing or saying something wrong without even knowing it. "Walking on eggshells" was a good descriptor for my school experience. I was delighted with the new age idea that children should be treated and spoken to like little adults, and that they would act accordingly.

I went in search of the lower school head to talk about what had happened the night before. Ms. K was the consummate school administrator, round-faced with snow-white short hair and crystal blue eyes that bored right into you. She was warm and kind but could be firm when the occasion demanded. Her voice had a whispered singsong quality, which always struck me as softening whatever message she needed to deliver to parents about their kids.

I was anxious to hear her reaction to Melissa's outburst, half hoping she would tell me it was normal for the new kindergartners to get nervous if there was something they didn't grasp right away. I finally tracked her down as she was herding third graders into assembly.

"Ms. K, I need to talk to you about Melissa," I said.

"What's up?" she asked, smiling with those blue eyes.

"She had a meltdown last night—it was totally unlike her. She told me she couldn't sound out a word the teacher had told the girls to sound out together. She said she didn't know what that meant, and all of the other girls did. Do you think she may already be having some reading problems?"

I was looking for the smile and response I wanted to hear, something that would reassure me that Melissa was just fine. Instead, Ms. K's face pinkened, her eyes got bright, and she said, "Good for you, Dewey, for getting on this so quickly. I will talk to her teacher and see what's up. We'll ask her to pay special attention to Melissa during the phonics lessons to see if she is getting it."

She didn't tell me not to worry. Instead, she ended by saying, "If there's a problem, we'll get right on it."

When I met with Ms. K again later that week, I told myself to relax.

"Dewey," she started. "Melissa's teacher agreed that there might be a problem with hearing the sounds of the letters, and she has offered to work with Melissa individually to get her caught up to the class. Can she come in a little early a couple of days a week?"

So, we began a new routine, with Melissa's school day starting early on Tuesdays and Thursdays so she could "work on her sounds." Melissa had a little smile on her face, showing how special she felt with this extra attention from her teacher.

But the next week, as Melissa bent over her homework one evening, she blurted, "Mommy, Ms. S made me go to the little house today and work with her. She took me out of class right during my favorite time when Ms. G was reading us a story about Mexico."

I forced myself to get more facts and to really listen, even though I knew that Ms. S was the learning specialist and was probably just doing periodic screenings to see if there had been any changes in Melissa's ability to hear simple sounds.

Then, Melissa said what would soon become a familiar refrain: "Why did she take *me* out and no one else, Mommy? Why don't the other girls have to go?"

"Maybe some of them will," I said, trying to sound unconcerned.

"But no one else has had to go! I would have seen them walking over there." Melissa was not lacking in persistence. Her eyes welled up. "Why am I the only one? Can you tell Ms. S to stop pulling me out of class?"

Self-Esteem and Learning Differences

If parents are blindsided when their kids are confronted with learning challenges, imagine the reaction of small children when they are suddenly aware that they can't do what their peers can. Self-esteem at any age is fragile. In the early years of school, when children are comparing themselves to their friends, listening to and sensing others' opinions of them, self-esteem is like brittle candy that can crack at a moment. All it takes is the slightest hint of disapproval or criticism. It is very painful for me, even now, to look back and think of how alone Melissa must have felt. Yet, she bravely got up every day and went to school for 4 long years. Knowing what I do now, I would never put a child through that again.

When Melissa's learning challenges first became apparent, everyone at the school talked to me about how self-esteem takes a hit when a child is singled out in a classroom for any reason. The message to the child is this: *You need special treatment. You can't keep up. You're not the same.* After a few weeks of this messaging, any child will begin to doubt themselves.

Not being able to read is one of the worst of these situations. It affects all of the other activities during school hours. There was no safe place where Melissa could hide her inability to read consistently—even on the playground, where the girls would use chalk on the blacktop to send each other messages.

Children cope with these challenges in different ways. Some sink into depression or withdraw, refusing to speak at school. For others, the best defense seems to be a bold offense. They begin to act out to distract from their academic difficulties. They may not even be conscious of this behavior, but it makes a kind of sense: *If I am being scolded for disrupting the class, no one will notice that I have no idea how to start my essay.*

Melissa was one of these kids. We had no idea what we were in for. I thought the academic challenges were tough, but they were just the beginning. Lacking the ability to control her academic destiny, she took control of anything else going on around her . . . in a negative way.

The social-emotional effects of struggling academically should never be ignored. In fact, many people who grapple with learning difficulties or attention issues are often labeled as depressed or afflicted with anxiety long before their specific learning differences can be explicitly identified. For example, one of the major indicators for an ADHD diagnosis is a history of social difficulties.

Acting Out From Discomfort

Ever since her personality had first begun to assert itself when she was 2, we had called Melissa our "pistol." This morphed into a special name given to her by her father, "La Pistola," our charming little weapon. But as the academic difficulties mounted, it seemed that her fiery personality was beginning to turn to trouble. She was impulsive, often writing on any books or papers she found, once even scrawling the word *Mom* on an antique wooden chest. She was constantly in motion, talking loudly enough to be disruptive most of the time. Her default answer to any plan was to say no, whether the suggestion was going out for a family dinner or playing with her friends.

I was slow to catch on to the pain behind these actions. Melissa was an outgoing and competitive child, so she externalized her fears and anxieties rather that internalizing them in the way other kids might. It's hard to admit to myself now, but the empathy that she so sorely needed escaped me for too long. Over time, my husband became her go-to person because he was more patient and steady.

Whenever Melissa was throwing a tantrum about the seams on her socks, hiding in the basement, or generally acting out, my reaction was to respond with unhelpful remarks like, "Why did you do that?" Of course, this sometimes led to screaming matches between us—a 50-year-old woman and her 6-year-old daughter. I am embarrassed even now to discuss these arguments, but I know that this situation goes on in other households, too. Talking about it is a helpful way to break the cycle.

Socially, Melissa was becoming stubborn and difficult, especially when playing a game with rules she couldn't read or follow—and sadly, there were many. Her competitive nature would cause her to cover up her mistakes with outlandish excuses, which basically came off as cheating. Soon, the other girls at her school began to tease and chastise her. This only caused her to ramp up her behavior.

We arranged to have Melissa tested for academic readiness and emotional maturity in December of that first year. The testing required two different sessions, but even the fact that she could skip 2 days of school did nothing to make her more cooperative. When we arrived at the test site, she refused to leave the car, not giving in until the test coordinator came out to extract her. Her obstreperousness was masking a deep fear of trying anything new that could possibly be added to her failures. I see this now, but at the time I thought she was simply being difficult.

One month later, my husband and I arrived at the educational therapist's office to hear the results of the testing. I was dreading the news. Would we hear that Melissa's IQ was not high enough to let her continue in this school? However, what we heard was not actually definitive enough to be of any real help.

"She's not really ready to attend school," the therapist began. "She is just not interested in learning yet." This, even though she was a full year older than most of the other girls in her class because the school had delayed her admission.

As for Melissa's IQ, the therapist said the tests were inconclusive. "She didn't really finish enough of the sections of the test to get a reliable score," she said. "But I can tell you she is very clever, obviously very smart. I can see this because of the ways she was able to *avoid* being tested. For example, in the opposites test, the instructions are to give a word that is the opposite of the word I said. And despite my repetition of this rule, Melissa continued to give me her version of an opposite. For 'hot,' she would say 'unhot.' She's a bright girl but needs more school readiness to really thrive."

I heard all of this and thought, *Well, of course. Difficult and obstinate behavior yet again.* I wasn't able to read between the lines: Melissa was stonewalling because she was so deeply sure she'd fail. She already had so little faith in herself.

In first and second grade, Melissa's self-esteem continued to slide. Her second-grade teacher, Ms. M, who had struggled with learning to read herself, identified and sympathized with Melissa's school difficulties. But sympathy did not seem to be enough. What Melissa needed at this point was real, authentic success in the classroom.

At that time, Melissa's teachers, even Ms. M, did not have adequate knowledge or experience in teaching children with dyslexia. In fact, no one was even willing to use the word *dyslexia* in any way—either as a diagnosis or as an explanation for Melissa's continued inability to develop reading and math skills despite the constant tutoring. The interventions she received were not adequate to correct the deficits she had in language arts. The adults around Melissa suffered from a lack of knowledge and experience, not a lack of caring. Still, she continued to lose ground to her peers.

On the playground and at soccer practice, Melissa's athletic talent allowed her to enjoy some success. But it wasn't enough to compensate for the other 6 hours in the day when she suffered from excruciating failure in the classroom. The disruptive behavior only worsened. The administrators and teachers shared that they were afraid that her self-esteem was getting so low that it might be time to change schools. This moment felt like a major defeat. I began to investigate other schools, but I was hampered by the fact that I didn't know what kind of school I should be looking for. I was afraid of jumping from the frying pan into the fire, knowing that any move would surely be disruptive to whatever little progress Melissa had made.

Then, one December afternoon, I got a call from Ms. K.

"Melissa's been stealing other girls' lunch cards," she said.

"Stealing?" I said. "Why on earth would she do that? We have plenty of money on her card. She can buy whatever she wants!"

The lunch cards were kept alphabetically in a rack in plain sight along the wall that led into the cafeteria. Each child could pick hers out on the way to the lunch line. Then, the cashier would look at the tray and deduct the proper amount from the advance payment each parent had put into an account. Apparently, Melissa had pulled someone else's card and used it in the line to pay for her tray. When the girl in question got to the rack of cards, she complained that hers was gone, and then someone noticed that Melissa was holding it.

I hung up the phone, took a deep breath, and felt a wave of shame roll through my body. "Melissa?" I called. "Can you explain this to me?"

She stood in front of me, tugging at her sweater collar—likely an itchy seam. Melissa was always complaining about tags, seams, and stitching as if they were torturing her.

"Why would you take another girl's lunch card?" I asked. "Especially when you have every ability to buy your own lunch?"

She shrugged and rolled her eyes. She had nothing to say.

It was only much later that I realized what had actually happened. I broke down in tears as the full impact of that moment hit me. There was a girl in the class named Rosie, and Melissa, in her heightened state of anxiety at not being able to read the names properly, had grabbed her card because it looked similar to her own last name, Rosetti. Melissa was so ashamed of her inability to read that she would rather be caught stealing than have it be discovered that she could not recognize her own name.

Doubts and Depression

Through all of this, Ms. K and the teachers made it clear that they really wanted to see my daughter succeed at the school. But I was beginning to doubt if they could. The school year ended with the usual conference, the same cast of people telling me what Melissa couldn't do. It was beginning to wear on me. Listening to the teachers and specialists rattle off the difficulties, infractions, and deficits, I couldn't help but wonder where I had gone wrong. It was dumbfounding; I had this wonderful child who seemed so normal on the outside yet was having profound difficulties in her daily life at school. Melissa was suffering from low self-esteem and the anxiety and depression that often accompany the inability to perform year after year.

I began to suffer from the same anxiety Melissa was experiencing, essentially for the same reasons: I felt out of control. There were no easy solutions, no surefire ways to help my child, and certainly no ways for her to help herself. My anxiety led to depression, which then turned into panic.

A friend suggested I seek therapy. The therapist he recommended was also a mother. "This woman is so normal and engaging," he told me. "I didn't even know for years that she was a psychologist." I knew what he meant. Many parents are suspicious of psychologists because of the old stereotype of a grim-faced professional sitting opposite a confused client, asking, "How does that make you feel?" Instead, I discovered that a well-trained psychologist can be very helpful in sorting out what lies at the root of anxiety and can point to solutions on how to move forward with positive action. I began to see this local psychologist once a week. These sessions proved to be just what I needed to help my family get unstuck on Melissa's problems.

Therapy made me face the reality that my parenting style with Melissa was very different than my husband's. "Get on the same page," the psychologist told me. "You're just confusing her with your different approaches." This psychologist helped me to see that Melissa's acting-out episodes were really just cries for help. Rather than scold her for bad behavior, I began to empathize with her for feeling like a misfit compared to her friends. My husband was instinctively much softer than I was, so I began to emulate his style.

My own sinking self-image and lack of confidence sent me into therapy in the first place, but this step was important for our family. A healthy self-image is crucial for any parent dealing with children. Strengthening my basic feelings of self-worth was an important step in moving forward.

Parents' self-esteem is tied up with their kids'. Fairly or not, society looks at a cooperative and polite child and thinks, *His parents did a great job with him; he knows how to behave so well.* Society sees an overachiever who cranks through long gymnastics practices and hours of Advanced Placement homework and thinks, *She's got a great work ethic; her parents obviously have a great approach.* The flip side of this coin is the screaming toddler, the video game zombie, or the antisocial teenager. The most common refrain you'll hear about these kids: *Where are the parents? They need to step up their game.*

Much has been written in recent years about competitive parenting, extreme mothering, and heightened expectations for middle-class and upper-middle-class families in today's world. If the parents of children who have few scholastic or social struggles still feel pressure to be "super parents," then the pressure on parents of children with learning differences is magnified tenfold.

When a child first presents with a learning challenge or behavior issue, parents are told that the child is broken and needs to be fixed. The child is given a diagnosis, just as they would receive with a chronic illness. The family then needs to work with therapists, specialists, and doctors and all of the language suddenly becomes medicalized. In this situation, it's difficult not to internalize the message that your child is damaged and that this is somehow your fault.

Parenthood often feels like one huge battle with the concept of control. Feeling in control can sometimes feel like being good at something. You can control what your children eat, what they watch on television, and what they wear to school. You can congratulate yourself on making choices that align with your values and seem to match up to society's expectations. But there are so many gray areas. You can't control your child's sleep patterns, height, or susceptibility to allergens. Even if you can control practice schedules and activity sign-ups, you can't control your child's athletic ability. You can't control your child's learning challenges either, although you can work tirelessly to mitigate them.

Feeling out of control feels a lot like being a bad parent. And feeling like a bad parent is a first-class ticket to depression, doubt, and self-sabotage. Additionally, for many parents, seeing a child's struggles can bring back painful memories of their own childhood issues. Many parents have self-esteem issues that have lingered for decades, rearing their heads when children confront the same challenges that parents struggled with years before.

I'm here to tell you that you're not a bad parent. The fact that you are taking action by reading this book and reflecting on your child's needs is proof that you're a caring, involved, hard-working parent.

Hitting Bottom

Finally, in March of her third-grade year, Melissa found the most dramatic of ways to tell my husband and I that she needed to get out of her school and that it had become a toxic environment for her. When I looked at the picture my daughter had drawn, with her holding a lit match to her school, I knew it was a cry for help. Something had to change, and to change dramatically.

Shortly after that incident, the school contracts for the following year came out. We didn't get one for Melissa. Instead, we discussed with the administration her need for a different learning environment.

Although Melissa was miserable at school, she was still upset when we made the decision to apply to alternative schools. We applied to several public and private schools and completed the rounds of interviews, our angry daughter in tow. She sabotaged most of the school visits by dressing absurdly, in either very tight or strange clothes, and acting sullen and noncompliant with us and the poor interviewers. I found myself making excuses. "Gosh," I'd say, a forced smile on my face. "She's just really having an off day today."

As I look back on these difficult visits, I feel a burden of guilt. I knew it was best for Melissa to leave her current school, but I was forcing my 8-year-old child to try to sell herself to school administrators with her sense of self-worth at rock bottom. At the same time, she clearly did not understand why she was leaving her school, even though she hated it and knew she hadn't been successful there.

When the school acceptance letters were sent out, our mailbox remained ominously empty. Then, a parade of dreaded thin envelopes arrived; not one school accepted Melissa, largely because I was naïve enough to include her test results with every application. No school, public or private, was willing to take on a child who couldn't read a word in the third grade and still had no official diagnosis of a learning difference.

But she had to attend school *somewhere*. After an agonizing search and countless conversations with specialists, there seemed to be no other choice: Melissa would have to go to a "special" school, one just for students with dyslexia.

I must admit I cringed at the idea; taking Melissa out of mainstream education felt like admitting defeat. But by that point, it was clear we had no other choice. The original path wasn't right for Melissa, so we would have to find another pathway to get her an education.

Reflection

Take a minute to jot down some incidents with your child that might be explained by a problem they are having in school. Describe the incidents. During a quiet moment, talk to your child about the possible reason for these incidents.

_____

_____

_____

_____

_____

_____

_____

_____

_____

_____

_____

_____

_____

CHAPTER 2

Turning the Tide

My husband and I saw a huge difference in approach at the Charles Armstrong School (CAS), where we sent Melissa after third grade. Despite our initial trepidation, the school was like a sudden breath of fresh air after years of living on tenterhooks.

The teachers were completely focused on the students, who came from all around the Bay Area for the school's innovative approach to educating students with learning difficulties. Although dyslexia was the main learning difference addressed, the school also dealt with other issues, like processing and attention problems, that are often associated with dyslexia. Beyond the desire to improve students' performance, teachers were committed to working with students' strengths.

This continuous positive feedback was a like a balm for Melissa. She needed to frequently hear about her own successes—perhaps as an antidote for the many reminders of her deficiencies that she'd received in previous years. With a new understanding of her strengths and new celebrations of her everyday triumphs, after a few months, Melissa began to relax into the comfort of believing in herself. Her newfound ease at school, and the surprising support of everyone around her, helped her begin to uncover a hidden truth that had been there all along: She was, in fact, capable of learning to read, not just haltingly, but with confidence and comprehension. She was buoyed by this knowledge, suddenly highly motivated to continue her progress. Except for the long commute—the school was nearly an hour from our home—Melissa never complained about going to CAS. What a change from her early elementary years!

Success at school for Melissa was all about finding the right fit. Whether by special training or by instinct, the CAS faculty were united in their efforts to make sure that the kids knew their strengths and were congratulated on their accomplishments every day or as often as possible. As a result, the atmosphere was more positive in that school community than in any other I had visited. This school was grounded in identifying patterns of strength and weakness in the whole child. The culture of the school focused on the well-being of the whole child, both in and out of the classroom. It wasn't just the power of positive thinking that made Melissa improve; the school actually used different techniques.

CAS also gave me the ability to work out my stress by volunteering at various tasks, each of which gave me more valuable insight into what kids with dyslexia were actually going through. Firsthand, I observed the strategies that the staff used to help kids. The experience was like total immersion in a new language, and I soaked it in.

Two-to-One Rule

The difference I saw in Melissa was the result of a strength-based approach, first used by a few teachers at CAS, and then adopted school-wide in Melissa's second year there. Together, the teachers and administrators created a new curriculum that incorporated each child's strengths inventory into the lesson plans.

This new approach affected the way I interacted with my family at home, and even the way I talked to myself about the things going on in my life. Dr. W, the head of school, championed the "two-to-one" rule: For every piece of constructive criticism, there should be two pieces of praise—not empty praise, but the kind that acknowledges grit, determination, and finding satisfaction in the process itself, not just the end result.

I recognized that too much criticism had been hard on my daughter's self-esteem—and on my own, too. I quickly adopted the two-to-one rule in my day-to-day communication and still use it today.

Finding Community

It didn't take long for my family to get thoroughly involved at CAS. My husband and I were encouraged to contribute by raising money, organizing the drama group, and even helping with real estate issues. Whatever the school needed, we wanted to help. This was the attitude of most of the parents there, and it was no surprise why. We were a community of parents who had suffered through some very painful moments when our kids found it difficult to succeed at previous schools, and we were all united in our relief at having landed in a safe haven for our kids and ourselves. We often turned to one another, talking about what really went on at home on bad days. It was a pleasure to be able to vent to another like-minded parent about troubles at home and have them validate the experience with one of their own.

The power of community is hugely important for parents struggling to come to terms with their child's learning challenges. More than any school's special education office, and more than any test or assessment, your community can reflect back your child's needs and illuminate your own. I had no idea how important a strong, supportive community really was until I was thrust into it and realized that there was no going back. I had the experience of the supportive folks at CAS, which planted the idea in my mind that a community of like-minded people is a must for families working with learning differences. I have also heard from many of the kids I encountered in the years since that being able to meet and get to know other kids who had some similar school issues helped with their confidence.

As I was to find out, school cultures can be challenged and changed through community action, from the individuals at the board level, to the parents, to the students and teachers. Most people in schools—educators and parents alike—are often still uneducated about learning challenges; that problem needs to be addressed by deploying persuasive facts at every level of the constituency. Changing an entrenched culture demands a complete overhaul of mindsets at every level of the community.

I also learned that parents and their kids have to take on the role of change-makers because they are basically the dissatisfied customers at the school. Teachers, administrators, and members of school boards, many of whom are parents whose children do not have learning differences, may not take up this fight on their own, as they do not have the self-interest to champion such an overhaul. In fact, teachers and administrators, overworked as they nearly always are, will often stand against change, not because they don't have each student's best interest at heart, but because they don't know what to do to help kids who need it.

As my mind and attitude about learning challenges changed, I began to speak up more. I talked endlessly to anyone who would listen about the educational landscape for kids who learned differently. I brought up this topic everywhere I went because I almost always found someone who wanted to talk about similar experiences. Sometimes these chats were fruitful, and people even thanked me for the tips I had shared. Sometimes, I suspect, I was just plain annoying to everyone around me.

I was eager to bring others into the discussion about the learning challenges their children were facing—not to embarrass anyone, but to acknowledge how many scared, frustrated, and desperate parents were really out there and to seek strength in our numbers. As more and more people opened up about their children's experiences, and as I delved deeper into my own research on different learning styles and individualized education, I felt more and more relief.

As I learned more about learning differences, I felt empowered. By studying methods of helping children with learning differences to work around their challenges, I found techniques that really worked to help kids succeed academically. Sharing real-life stories with others about what had worked, what hadn't worked, and what resources were available gave me hope. My anxiety receded with every anecdote and every compassionate hug.

Of course, it wasn't all encouraging. The more of these conversations I had, the more I realized that many people—parents, teachers, and even learning specialists—were hearing confusing or contradictory messages about what could be done to help struggling kids. Schools were often inconsistent in their approach. For instance, a teacher might challenge a student on accommodations (e.g., extra time to take a test, having a reader, using a calculator, or being able to listen to a book on tape for content and analysis) that had been recommended by a specialist within that same school. It wasn't always easy to know which advice to take and what the most current thinking was.

I needed to know more.

Conference Crawler

The Charles Armstrong School taught me one key lesson: In order for me to gain back control, I needed to understand my daughter as a learner. The faculty took the time to really *know* my child. I thought that if they could do that in the school, I could certainly do it at home. But in order to create the right environment for Melissa to flourish, I needed to learn more about learning differences myself.

I became a regular at a variety of different conferences and workshops. I will never forget my first national conference, a 3-day event put on in the early 2000s by the Learning Disabilities Association (LDA) in Denver. There were several thousand people in attendance from all over the country, and from many different disciplines, as well as a large number of parents. I was in heaven for 3 days, awed by all of the information available on my new passion. There were speakers who addressed every topic, from ADHD to dyslexia, to the behavioral problems that resulted from having students with these differences in the classroom. The bookstore alone was enough to send me reeling. I wanted every book I could see, in case it had one sentence that would afford me a sliver of insight into how to help my child. I spent an obscene amount of money on books at that first conference. I became the talk of the booksellers, who speculated on whether I was planning to open my own bookstore.

I was enthralled when I surrounded myself with these treasured resources after I got back home. It calmed me just to have this information at hand, even if I couldn't possibly read it all. Merely having access to answers made me feel proactive and in charge.

Even before I went to the large conference, I found my way to a much smaller local conference put on by the foundation created by Charles Schwab, the well-known financier. He himself has dyslexia, and his family foundation has provided help to parents and teachers, including sponsoring several conferences related to learning issues. In 1996, the keynote speaker at the Schwab Foundation's conference in San Francisco was a young author and motivational speaker, Rick Lavoie. I went through a whole pack of tissues during his talk. His words resonated so deeply, and the timing couldn't have been better for me. I was just coming to terms with Melissa's assessment results, and school was still immensely challenging for her. I was feeling overwhelmed and exhausted by trying to meet my daughter's particular needs.

Lavoie is a born storyteller who can turn an anecdote about a student or a parent he has known into a moving lesson about parenting, learning, and getting by in a world that is just not set up for these challenges. He captured my attention that day with just a few words: "One of the most frightening things a parent can hear is that her child has a learning disability" (Reading Rockets, 2018). Of course, I knew exactly what he meant—the dying of the dream, the dark fears for the future.

Lavoie compared navigating a learning disability diagnosis to trying to get out of a waterbed: "You're flailing around, looking for something solid, trying to prop yourself up, but there's just no firm ground to push against" (Reading Rockets, 2018). He spoke of the conflicts that stakeholders navigate: parents disagreeing with teachers and therapists, parents and children clashing, and parents fighting one another over new approaches and strategies. "You're not fighting because you're mad at the kid," he said. "You're fighting because you're grieving." I knew that grief all too well.

Perhaps the biggest takeaway from this presentation was Lavoie's way of comparing a child's self-esteem to a cup of poker chips. "Each child," he said, "is born with a cup that has a certain number of chips to start with. As the child grows up, everything she does and sees and hears and experiences either adds to or subtracts from that store of chips. Problems at school cause a steady drop in chips, as do negative interactions with other kids, and with parents" (Reading Rockets, 2018).

As he spoke, I realized with sadness how many chips Melissa had lost on a daily basis at her old school. As she looked around the classroom and compared herself to the other girls, her stockpile of chips dwindled. Worse, her measly store was depleted even further when I yelled at her and vented my frustration. Guilt came crashing down around me as I thought about the ways I'd mishandled conflict over the years. As the stakes at school had increased, I had put more pressure on her when I should've been applying less. It was a major revelation—one I'm glad I had at that point, early enough in our relationship that I could try to change our dynamic. I resolved to fill her chip cup as much as I could.

In the years since, I have never stopped learning about the cutting-edge techniques and strategies being published by experts in the educational field. See the Recommended Resources section of this book for brief summaries of the work of the most useful writers I have encountered.

From Convert to Missionary

At the Charles Armstrong School, the idea that accommodations had to be tailored to the needs of the individual had already been widely adopted. But I was concerned that this vital knowledge wasn't being shared with the wider world. Every day, I saw parents and friends with kids struggling in mainstream schools, where teachers didn't necessarily understand that a kid with learning differences might need a little extra time or a separate space to take a test.

Then, an idea hit me: Teachers and school administrations would change their thinking if they just knew what I had learned in my deep dive into the world of learning differences. Believing as I always have that educators, just like parents, want the best for their students, I decided the problem must be a lack of information.

On an impulse, I called two women who had been the original educational consultants to diagnose my daughter. I considered them both to be my mentors, as they had guided me every step of the way in getting accommodations for Melissa and had attended school conferences with me. I proposed a gathering at my house with some of their colleagues. I shared that I wanted to start an organized effort to bring schools and parents in our city together to collaborate on helping kids with learning differences.

At that point, I had no definite vision; I just explained to my mentors how discouraging and lonely it was for so many parents to keep having the same conversations, again and again, with teachers. I told them how frustrating it could be that even when parents had the information they needed to help their kids thrive, there was no system in place for informing and connecting everyone involved in the process.

So, I proposed that they both come to my house and discuss with other professionals how we might change this dynamic. I also intended to invite some committed and knowledgeable parents to this meeting, but I wanted to be careful that the gathering wouldn't devolve into a complaint session for frustrated and angry parents. Rather, I wanted this to be a problem-solving session with experts.

Not only did my mentors immediately agree, but they also referred me to some of their colleagues whom they urged me to invite. We made a shortlist of names and settled on a date in February 2002 for the first meeting. Looking back, that call seems like the founding moment of the Parents Education Network (PEN), the organization we would go on to formally establish the following year with the help of numerous parents, educators, and advisors, including cofounder Sandy Otellini, a friend whose child also attended the Charles Armstrong School.

From our first conference in 2003, to 2017 when PEN merged with a much larger organization (Children's Health Council, in Palo Alto), PEN became the go-to source for reliable information on learning differences from nationwide experts from a variety of fields, all of whom were selected for the insights they shared with parents about how to help their kids navigate schools. In 15 years, PEN's programs grew to include peer groups for parents, kids, teachers, learning specialists, and more than 150 schools, not only in the Bay Area but also in three other cities. The annual conference we designed was held for 11 years at the San Francisco Giants' Stadium and became nationally known and attended by parents, teachers, school administrators, learning specialists, and kids who have a learning difference. It became PEN's trademark as a unique way to bring all those interested in helping kids with learning differences.

Through PEN I became connected with a new movement in education, neuroscience, and psychology, spearheaded by Todd Rose, a high school dropout who found his way to becoming a professor at Harvard's Graduate School of Education and the head of the Mind, Brain, and Education Department there. I then cofounded an organization with Rose called Populace, which stresses the importance of understanding each individual's learning profile and areas of strength and weakness in order to maximize the potential in every learner.

Not all parents can simply change schools or find a game changer like CAS in their area. The rest of this book is designed to act as a guidebook to help you better understand and help your child thrive, no matter what school they attend. I have distilled the ideas of key thinkers and cutting-edge experts, as well as my own decades of experience, into universally applicable steps that will work with every child to reinforce their strengths while minimizing their weaknesses.

Reflection

Jot down the names of people in your child's life who appreciate your child's personality. Think about how to put your child into more situations with these adults and kids who bring out the best in your child.

Then, think about who in your own circle of friends is the most accepting of your family situation. Who really listens to your worries and offers positive insight? Make more time for these people to surround yourself with positivity.

_____

_____

_____

_____

_____

_____

_____

_____

_____

_____

_____

_____

_____

_____

_____

Part II

Changing the Mindset

CHAPTER 3

Mindset Is Key

When my anxiety about Melissa's academic difficulties was mounting, I didn't realize that I was largely responsible for the negativity I felt about her future. Although I wasn't conscious of it at the time, my own fixed mindset about intelligence, success, and achievement proved to be every bit as challenging as her learning differences.

Stanford psychology researcher Carol Dweck (2006/2016) brought the idea of mindset into the national conversation with her book *Mindset: The New Psychology of Success.* Mindset is frequently discussed in conversations about parenting children with learning challenges. A fixed mindset, specifically, is the enemy of all individuals striving for success, but it is particularly toxic for parents of kids who learn differently. Dweck's research showed that students who thought of their talents and abilities as inborn and fixed were limiting their efforts to try new challenges and take risks that might improve their abilities. A fixed mindset can also contribute to a very narrow definition of success: perfect SAT scores, Ivy League schools, and a white-collar career. Growth mindsets encourage greater achievement borne of risk-taking and learning from failure.

When parents have a fixed mindset about their child's achievement, they can unintentionally disadvantage their kids even more. Parents may look at a child's mathematical struggles and think: *Well, it looks like math is not her thing. I'd better steer her away from that engineering career and into the social sciences.* Instead of tackling kids' weaknesses with a can-do attitude, fixed mindset parenting assumes that kids are only good at certain things.

In fixed mindset thinking, the talents one is born with are fixed; therefore, if a child is born with a brain that struggles with learning to read, this can be a death sentence to success in most parents' minds. Certainly, most parents of a child with dyslexia would discourage their child's pursuit of a writing career, yet a surprising number of famous authors do indeed have dyslexia, as you will see in later chapters of this book.

This mindset idea works another way, too. Many parents become adamant that the area in which their child shows the most talent is the pathway their child should choose as a passion. But then, to their befuddlement, such parents often watch their child switch from a career that seems predestined by talent to one less obvious; the child is more excited by another path, even if it requires more training or harder work.

As I compared Melissa to the other kids around her and despaired at what she couldn't do, I was missing the things she could do. I saw the milestones she hadn't hit yet, and in my fixed mindset, I read this as a sign that she must not be as "smart" as I had hoped she would be. This fear paralyzed me. Instead of taking action to get Melissa the help she needed, I waited. (What I was waiting for, I didn't know.)

I unfairly equated a slow start in school with a slow finish as an adult. I was doing her, and myself, a grave disservice. I needed to pivot from a fixed mindset to a growth mindset to truly see this. I discovered this is a journey and not a switch to flip.

From Fixed to Growth Mindset

In a growth mindset, according to Dweck (2006/2016), the challenge and process of learning is as valuable as the end result. Figuring out new strategies is the pathway to success. A growth mindset helps kids understand that real achievement almost never happens without a great deal of effort and learning. For parents, a growth mindset means looking for ways to help kids develop their skills, seeking out novel methods that work for each individual child, and avoiding the "I guess you're just not a math/English/science person" thinking trap.

Embracing a growth mindset can mean challenging your assumptions about the "correct" way to do something and the "proper" place for learning. The school where Melissa began her education did not set up her up for success. She needed a school that would respect her learning style and pace instead of shaming her for it. She needed the kind of praise that helps a growth mindset to flourish:

- "Your brain is growing while you work on those math problems!"
- "Every time you practice your handwriting, it looks a little neater. And your hands are growing stronger, too."
- "I can tell that reading this book is hard for you, but you are learning how to recognize some really big words. Isn't that exciting?"

It would be several more years before I understood how my fixed mindset was contributing to Melissa's troubles. For decades I had believed that intelligence and academic potential were fixed, finite, and definable in a narrow way. "Smart" meant good grades, high test scores, and quick thinking. "Success" meant stellar report cards, fat envelopes from the best schools, and job titles and salaries that had cachet.

It was an unexpected relief when my original mindset was finally challenged. Slowly, I realized that my lifelong conviction that a person was born with a fixed amount of "smarts" and potential was completely false and actually harmful to my daughter's self-esteem.

Mindset isn't a switch that can be flipped—it takes a lot of work to make that mental shift. But I believe it is the important first step that you must make as a parent of a child with learning differences. Evolving from a fixed to a growth mindset helps you see not just what is "wrong" with your child, but what is right, what is challenging, and what is possible.

What Is Your Mindset?

People are often completely unaware of their mindset until something happens to challenge it. This was demonstrated to me when my daughter's learning differences were first brought to light. Part of my devastation had to do with worrying that she was not smart. At the time, my definition of "smart" was a product of my fixed mindset; I thought that people were born with a predetermined amount of intelligence and that there wasn't much people could do to boost that innate level of brain power. I had a rigid image of what successful education looked like: breezing through elementary and secondary school, collecting accolades on the way to a top-tier college, followed by graduate school.

I can look back now and see what slowly changed my mindset about Melissa's learning strengths. It was the transformation of so many kids at the Charles Armstrong School, from anxious, depressed, and lacking confidence about their abilities, to thriving, eager-to-learn, happy kids. One salient example was in CAS's renowned drama department, which was led by an athletic coach with dyslexia who had found sports and acting to be cathartic outlets for him as a young student. Kids would perform in the annual show, and often parents were flabbergasted by the unexpected singing and acting talent of their own children. Success stories of kids like mine shifted my mindset about how to succeed in life. This realization changed my way of relating to people; indeed, it changed my self-image as well.

It took time, research, support, and community, but I slowly came to embrace a growth mindset. I saw that my daughter was able to master difficult things when she tried new methods and didn't give up. I became aware of the power of perseverance and saw that there were so many ways to embody "smart" and "successful." It wasn't an easy journey, but I'm grateful that our challenges with Melissa's schooling led to my development of a growth mindset. I tap into it all of the time, whether looking at my family or myself.

Perhaps you can think of a fixed mindset you once held and now view very differently because your life experience proved you wrong.

Confounding Low Expectations

A perfect example of a fixed mindset came to my attention after Melissa started college. A friend of mine had made a new acquaintance, a retired tutor and learning specialist who had once worked at Melissa's elementary school. As they chatted, they became aware that they both knew our family. My friend excitedly reported the great news about Melissa being a student and athlete at the University of California, Berkeley, now in her sophomore year. To her dismay, and later to mine, the tutor was adamant that Melissa could not have gotten into a Division I athletic school and one of the foremost public universities in the county, which was very selective in its admissions process. She insisted to my friend that it must have been one of the California State universities, whose admission policies were more lenient, as Melissa wasn't smart enough, in her opinion, to get into a top-notch school.

When my friend relayed this story to me, I remembered that years before, we had switched to a different tutor because my daughter was not comfortable with the original one provided by the school—this same woman whose mindset was so fixed she simply could not believe the success my daughter had enjoyed. Melissa had never connected with her, and I could now see that children can tell when adults have a closed mind about their abilities.

Learning to Fail Better

One of the cornerstones of a fixed mindset is the fear of failure and being humiliated. People with a fixed mindset often believe that intelligence or success means never making mistakes. In a growth mindset, success is about learning and practicing until mastery is achieved.

One of Dweck's (2006/2016) studies of children as young as 4 demonstrated the difference between kids with growth and fixed mindsets. She offered children an easy puzzle, and when they completed it successfully, she asked if they'd like to do the easy puzzle again or if they would like a more challenging puzzle. The kids with a fixed mindset chose the easy puzzle—it was "safe," and they knew they wouldn't make a mistake. The kids with a growth mindset chose the challenge. For them, success wasn't about getting everything right, it was about stretching themselves. They would ask questions such as, "Why would anyone want to do the same puzzle over and over?"

The Power of (the Right Kind of) Praise

Elsewhere in this book, I've discussed the important role that building self-esteem plays in creating a positive parent-child relationship, especially when learning differences are present. Most parents know that they are uniquely positioned to bolster their children's confidence, and that encouragement and praise can help kids feel good about themselves. But there's a caveat: Parents' instinct to praise their child's abilities and traits can cause more harm than good *if the praise is not authentic.* To foster a growth mindset, parents must use the right kind of praise.

One of Dweck's (2006/2016) studies into mindset and its effect on children demonstrated what kind of praise works best. In the study, Dweck and her researchers presented 10-year-olds with a fairly simple puzzle. Most of the kids solved it easily. Some of the children were given feedback such as, "Wow, you're good at this! You must be really smart." This type of feedback praises *intelligence.* Other children were told, "Great! You must have worked really hard at that." This feedback praises *effort,* which is not an inherent trait. The study's findings were startling: Kids who were praised for intelligence were more likely to cheat on future tests in order to save face, choose "easy" tests over more difficult ones, and do poorly on future tests at the same level. On the other hand, kids who were praised for effort relished challenging tasks, even those that were designed to make them fail. They were more likely to keep trying when presented with a difficult test and more likely to improve their scores over time. Dweck (2014) called this the power of "yet." Kids with a growth mindset are more likely to believe that they can improve, and even if they can't do something right away, that just means they can't do it *yet.* They are more motivated to try different methods to get to a solution, and they are more likely to enjoy the bumpy road to success.

It may seem simple to make the shift from saying, "You're so talented/ smart/good at this," to "You tried so hard/were really working/didn't give up." But it's hard, especially when kids who learn differently always feel like they're struggling and unable to catch up. The results, though, are worth the effort. Sometimes, finding an activity that provides an inroad to a growth mindset can help kids broaden their mindset to other areas of life. Something low-stakes, like an art class or a new sport, can help kids see that practice and effort can pay off.

Effort Combined With Learning

Several years after *Mindset's* initial publication in 2006, Dweck (2015) began to see that there was a need for some addenda and corrections to her theories. Growth mindset theory had become widely known in more progressive education circles, and many parents were learning about the perils of the wrong kind of praise. However, Dweck saw that many well-intentioned people were misusing her theory, leading to even more problems with kids' self-esteem.

Dweck (2015) wrote that many people were *only* praising effort. Even when a student failed, they were saying things like, "You tried really hard!" They were missing a key element: a focus on the resulting learning. Dweck wrote, "We also need to remember that effort is a means to an end to the goal of learning and improving" (para. 6).

Effort doesn't mean anything if there is never any improvement. Teachers and parents need to pull all of these elements together, emphasizing that the process of learning is the combination of the attempt, the effort, and the end result. Effective praise acknowledges that the child's mistakes are part of the process of learning. Unhelpful praise merely rewards the student for trying. There's a big difference.

Changing your mindset requires a leap of faith, but it's one of the most critical steps to becoming an effective and supportive parent to a child who learns differently. When everyone is using a growth mindset, parents and children can work together through challenges toward triumph. Failure will be part of the process, but when you know it's not the end, you can find the strength to keep going.

Reflection

Think about some fixed mindsets that you once held. What caused you to change your thinking? Do you have a fixed mindset about IQ or talent? If so, what have you learned in this chapter to help you broaden your thinking?

_____

_____

_____

_____

_____

_____

_____

_____

_____

_____

_____

_____

_____

CHAPTER 4

The Deceptive
Language of Disability

It's easy to beat myself up when I look back at how readily I initially accepted the labeling of my daughter as "learning disabled." How could I have been so closed-minded? Why, when I heard the term *learning disability* in reference to my child, did I really hear *inability to learn*? But considering how learning challenges have been viewed over time, I was working not only against my own prejudices, but also against centuries of confusion, misguided crusades, and outright falsities surrounding these issues. Sadly, many of the doctors and therapists who set out to assist children with learning challenges actually made the experience more difficult in the long term, as they focused on deficiencies and discrepancies rather than relative strengths.

Like most parents, I not only accepted, but also welcomed the diagnosis of dyslexia to explain Melissa's difficulties learning in a mainstream classroom. Unfortunately, at the time (and even today) an educational assessment and accompanying diagnosis was necessary to get accommodations and school support. A diagnosis is a medical term that describes what is wrong with a person that needs to be cured or fixed. This evaluation usually leads to a label like dyslexia, ADHD, or ASD. Not only are these labels nondescriptive of any one individual, but they can also be very damaging to a student's self-esteem. Teachers and others invariably make assumptions about what these children can and can't do because of the label they've been given.

Some forward-thinking scientists, doctors, and educators are finally moving away from this disability-based approach. In order to fight back against this language, it is helpful to review how the outmoded disability model began.

The History of Learning Differences

What did Charles Darwin, Isaac Newton, Albert Einstein, George Washington, and Agatha Christie all have in common? They all had what would today be called learning differences.

Darwin, one of the most revolutionary scientific thinkers ever to have lived, recalled toward the end of his life that he had always been considered a "very ordinary boy below the common standard in intellect" (Masters in Special Education, 2019). In later life, he was constantly upbraided by his sister for his atrocious spelling.

Experts believe that both Einstein and Newton—who together revolutionized the field of physics—showed clear signs of Asperger's syndrome, a form of autism that often confers a great talent for grasping complex systems but can also make people socially awkward and experience problems communicating (Masters in Special Education, 2019).

Washington, another notoriously bad speller, may well have suffered from dyslexia, while Christie became the world's foremost crime writer of her day despite the fact that she likely suffered from dysgraphia, which affects a person's penmanship and ability to spell (Masters in Special Education, 2019). Christie simply dictated most of her novels, spinning her complex plot lines and characters in her head.

However, none of these figures were diagnosed with a condition because when they were alive there was little understanding of the different ways that children could learn—even children who would grow up to become world-changers. Historically, in education, difference has long been persecuted instead of celebrated.

Western culture once equated difference—any kind of difference, from mental illness, to epilepsy, to physical deformity—with a kind of moral failing on the part of the child or a divine punishment for the moral failings of the family. If a child couldn't sit still, pay attention, or learn at the same rate as their siblings, this could only mean that the child was wicked, and therefore must be punished and/or tamed. If a child was disorganized or prone to daydream, they were considered lazy and useless.

There are no records of any meaningful study or discussion of learning problems until the middle of the 19th century. Before the Industrial Revolution, education was mostly the realm of the elite, and literacy was not widespread in the general population. As a broader population became educated in an organized, standardized way—largely in response to the needs of nation states' growing bureaucracies and industries—it became clear that learning challenges of various kinds were present in a sizeable percentage of students. Popular thinking assigned the fault of the challenges to the individuals with the differences, instead of to the shortcomings of the system of learning developed around the notion of one-size-fits-all.

Well into the 20th century, kids who struggled with reading or with attention were segregated from the general student populations. Children were often misdiagnosed as "mentally deficient" and stigmatized for their entire lives.

A New Term, New Services, and New Stigmas

The term *learning disabled* was coined in 1963 by Samuel Kirk, a professor in special education at the University of Illinois. Kirk first used the term in a presentation on so-called "perceptually handicapped" children. Working with a group of concerned parents, Kirk proposed that many children in special education seemed to need a different descriptor. They were not "mentally retarded," but seemed to have "disorders in development of language, speech, reading, and associated communication skills," as he put it.

Kirk helped found the Association for Children with Learning Disabilities. He wanted these children to get services that would assist them in public schools—services different from those offered to kids with debilitating intellectual disabilities. Through his efforts, the U.S. government eventually did mandate services for "learning disabled" students through acts like the Americans With Disabilities Act (ADA) of 1990 and the Individuals With Disabilities Education Act (IDEA).

Although Kirk and his colleagues had many good intentions behind establishing the ADA and IDEA, they drew from the deficit approach to learning; they believed that kids who learn differently are damaged, sick, or somehow "less than." The language of disability is a language steeped in judgment.

Although ADA and IDEA helped to get kids accommodations in the classroom, such as extra time to take tests and access to the resources they needed, these acts did not close the gap sufficiently, as any parent of a child with learning challenges, particularly in a typical public school, can tell you. IDEA does not explicitly state that the schools have a responsibility to help students reach their maximum potential. The implication here is that a passing grade is acceptable to meet the requirements of the law. As more than one principal has told me, "It's not my job to get these students A grades. It's my job to help them obtain an average education . . . in other words, C's." This average education is not what parents should be settling for.

Under the current educational system, such labels are sometimes necessary bureaucratic measures to unlock the tools your child will need to access. Parents should by no means throw out the baby with the bathwater. However, you must never let these labels seep into your mindset or affect how you see your child, and certainly never let it color your child's view of themselves.

More Than One Way to Learn

Just decades after the language of disability began to spread, psychologists and educators were beginning to fight against it. In 1983, Howard Gardner, a professor of education at Harvard, developed his theory of multiple intelligences. Although it did not specifically address learning difference issues, this theory had a major impact on educational theory overall. Gardner (1983/2011) challenged the idea that intelligence could be measured and represented by one number. He put forth the idea that there are many different types of intelligence, including musical, interpersonal, intrapersonal, mathematical, spatial, verbal, and physical. This thinking gave way to the belief that people's types of intelligence could perhaps account for different learning styles, like auditory, kinesthetic, and visual. This way of thinking helped classrooms become more accessible to all children's learning styles and paved the way for more successful classroom inclusion for kids who learn differently.

Another researcher, Mel Levine, began applying this type of thinking to education in the late 1980s and early 1990s. Levine's organization, All

Kinds of Minds, campaigned to develop richer school standards to help evaluate learners of all kinds, not just verbal and mathematical learners. All Kinds of Minds (2019) stated,

> We celebrate personal uniqueness in so many places, and yet our schools still follow a factory model that forces both teachers and students into routines that engage and reward certain learners while marginalizing others. . . . strengths, weaknesses, and affinities shape both *how we learn* and *what engages us*—which in turn both influence how much we actually learn and thrive in a given situation. (paras. 5–6)

Levine's work was groundbreaking in its message that all children could learn—they simply need the right learning language to be successful.

See Figure 1 for a quick review of attitudinal changes toward learning differences over the years.

Testing: An Assessment or a Diagnosis?

There came a point in the early days of Melissa's schooling when the tense meetings with teachers and administrators led to the subject of official disability testing. I remember that telltale blush creeping over Ms. K's face as we began to discuss the pros and cons of having Melissa officially assessed.

"A diagnosis can be the first step to making real strides," she said. I remember thinking that she used the same hushed, fervent tones that people use with the parents of sick children. Of course, the language used is often the language of illness: *disability, testing, diagnosis, treatment.*

If you do decide to test your child's abilities, there are a number of factors to consider.

The Psych-Ed Report

The Psychological Education Assessment Report (psych-ed report) is a tool that was designed to show a person's weaknesses in areas of learning and academic subjects. It also shows a pattern of strengths, but unfortu-

FIGURE 1
Evolution of Attitudinal Changes Toward Learning Differences

Pre 1960	Learning differences are seen as a moral failing, a punishment to the family, or "mental retardation."
1963	Kirk coins the term *learning disability*, leading to a medical model of brain function variability; aligned with the disability movement.
1980s–1990s	Gardner develops the theory of multiple intelligences. Levine further defines different dimensions of intelligence. All Kinds of Minds is born.
2006	Dweck publishes *Mindset*, introducing the concept of fixed and growth mindsets to challenge the notion that intelligence is a fixed trait.
2016	Rose publishes *The End of Average* to challenge the traditional thinking that there is an average intelligence.

nately many clinicians, schools, and teachers focus solely on the areas of deficit because the test is used to qualify a student for special education classes and accommodations in public schools.

The report is based on a discrepancy model. This means that the child's intelligence, or IQ, is tested first with a battery of tests, including verbal and spatial reasoning, sequencing, and logic, to see how the child performs on each type of task. Then, the student's achievement is tested in the subjects of math, reading, writing, etc. The scores for each learning area are subtracted from the IQ score to see if there is a gap between the two, which is often the first indicator of a learning difference. The scores are averaged for a "full-scale IQ," which is only seen as a guideline, not an absolute.

For some students, the results of this kind of evaluation can be, at worst, inaccurate and, at best, misleading. Some evaluations are helpful and descriptive, but others are either too vague, giving average scores in most areas, or dwell on deficits instead of balancing the picture between strengths and challenges. In Melissa's case, all of her evaluations were pretty useless in understanding how to work with her, or how bright and talented she was.

Recently, the validity of these types of test results has been questioned because the normed scores are based on an average student in each age group—a ranking system that is becoming less and less trusted as an indication of individual abilities. As Rose (2016) has discussed, average does not describe anyone as an individual. When the majority of society can accept that there is no such thing as an "average" student, surely a replacement system of measurement of aptitude and ability will follow. But until then, educators and parents need to use these measures as best they can.

In most public school districts, children are not eligible for testing unless academic or behavioral problems have persisted for years. By that time, of course, the damage to self-esteem for both parent and child has already been done, and everyone is likely feeling anxious and upset. These stressors may interfere measurably with the child's performance on the tests.

As an example of how inadequate this kind of testing might be for parents to determine their child's unique profile of strengths and weaknesses, Figure 2 shows Melissa's testing, which stayed substantially the same from her first testing at age 6 to her last assessment at 18 before she went to college.

The results show that her higher order cognition measured in the "low average" to "average" range, while all of her achievement scores (mastered skills in reading, math calculation, and writing) were in that same range. Her relative strengths, as shown in the report, were in vocabulary, social skills, motor skills, and muscle memory. Her executive function skills, such as organization and planning, were her highest, on the high average range. Melissa was never able to complete some sections of each test due to her difficulties with reading and writing, which automatically caused her high anxiety and interfered with her performance. After the first of these evaluations, my husband and I never paid much attention to the IQ or intellectual predictions made by the subsequent tests she needed to take in order to qualify for accommodations at school, nor to the standardized tests for high school and college.

Over time different evaluators identified different strengths by reading Melissa's history of activities and talking to teachers and to Melissa herself, including:

- organization and planning;

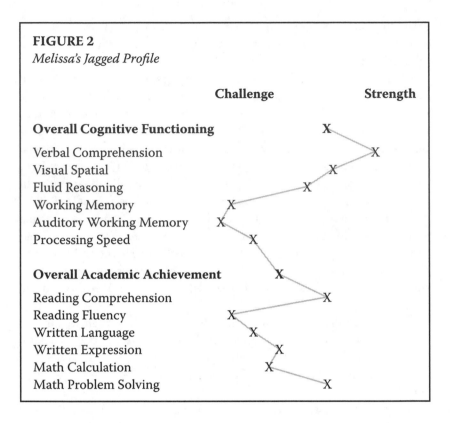

FIGURE 2
Melissa's Jagged Profile

	Challenge	Strength
Overall Cognitive Functioning		X
Verbal Comprehension		X
Visual Spatial		X
Fluid Reasoning	X	
Working Memory	X	
Auditory Working Memory	X	
Processing Speed	X	
Overall Academic Achievement	X	
Reading Comprehension		X
Reading Fluency	X	
Written Language	X	
Written Expression	X	
Math Calculation	X	
Math Problem Solving		X

- social skills;
- well-placed humor;
- effort and motivation;
- artistic expression—drawings, dressing, decorating;
- color sense;
- mental strength, especially in sports;
- sensitivity and empathy; and
- athleticism.

Melissa's assessments might have discouraged us from even suggesting that she go to college, had we paid more attention to the low scores during the early school years. Her weaknesses in the classroom pointed to failure, and if we had focused on that without taking her strengths outside of the classroom into account, it could have become a self-fulfilling prophecy. We were lucky to have sound advice from experienced and educated teachers and professionals, who were always impressed by Melissa's intangible strengths, like perseverance, competitiveness, and drive, which established her strong work ethic from an early age. Focusing on strengths points toward the path to success. Why shouldn't these strengths be the areas of focus?

The first time I held Melissa's academic assessment in my shaking hands, I had no idea what I was looking at. Most parents have the same experience. I skimmed a lot of the jargon, looking for the specific elements that I could make sense of. Entire books have been written to explain how to read these reports. Only some professionals are qualified to administer and interpret the findings from the tests contained in the evaluation, and the type of degree the evaluators hold determines which tests they can administer.

Adding to the complexity of the whole process, the quality of the results depends heavily on the interactions between the evaluator and the client, the observations made by the evaluator while asking the questions, and the state of mind of the person being assessed. If your child isn't comfortable during the testing sessions, which are usually performed over 2 days, or if they are sick or stressed, the outcome will be skewed.

Testing for Assessment of Abilities

Many testing instruments have been developed over the years, mostly by psychologists, that are designed to assess a student's abilities in different parts of the brain. A psychoeducational exam, or psych-ed assessment, is done to determine a child's whole learning profile (i.e., strengths and weaknesses in potential as well as achievement). The psych-ed report must be administered and written by a licensed psychologist and is used to determine a child's need for accommodations. In California, it is no longer legal to administer IQ tests based on verbal abilities, because the language-based questions automatically discriminate against children from low-income families. Any kind of one-on-one evaluation or assessment is expensive and can range anywhere from $2,500 to $5,000. Some clinics will provide the service for a reduced fee on a sliding scale based on family income. Public schools are required to provide an educational evaluation if the child has exhibited inability to stay at grade level, over an extended period of time, depending on the state.

The psych-ed report and the even more comprehensive neuro-psych assessment are just snapshots of a moment in time. They can give you a good idea of what your child might struggle with, and where they can excel, but they are not the be-all and end-all for understanding your child. Schools and specialists are finally accepting this fact. A friend of mine recently showed me her daughter's psych-ed report, which had been administered by a school psychologist employed by the public school district. The report contained this statement: "Please keep in mind that these tests are merely a snapshot in time. A child's performance and scores can vary from day to day depending on many different factors, and his or her abilities and challenges may change over time."

Appendix B contains a sample psych-ed evaluation report with relevant sections and scores highlighted.

Context Is Key

Private schools expect parents to pay for the ability assessment. Luckily, my husband and I were able to hire a private psychiatrist who came highly recommended by the school, and she steered us toward highly trained and experienced professionals for the initial testing. But Melissa's results were as inconsistent as she was and showed very little about how to help her.

The most important aspect of her original assessment, however, was the experience of the testers and the psychiatrist's interpretation and guidance that accompanied the report. The two people I used each had 30 years of experience with kids, teachers, and administrators from the local independent schools. They were able to recommend appropriate schools and programs unique to my child.

SELECTING A PSYCHOLOGIST FOR YOUR CHILD

Because of the complexity of the assessments, and the specific education required to perform them, I asked a renowned Bay Area neuropsychologist, Dr. Leyla Bologlu, to provide a list of questions parents should ask when selecting a psychologist to evaluate their child. This is the information she provided (personal communication, October 2016):

1. **Parents should feel free to ask professionals about their training, background, and area of expertise.** There are different

kinds of professionals who do testing: master's level educational specialists, psychologists (Ph.D.), and neuropsychologists (Ph.D. plus). Parents should know who they are seeing. Regardless of the educational background, a state license is required.

2. **Parents should ask the clinician to provide a bullet-pointed outline of strengths, weaknesses, and recommended interventions as part of the report.** The goal is to provide a document that will enable parents to advocate for their child. This is a difficult task given the number of different professionals who will read the report (e.g., parents, schools, therapists, tutors, occupational therapists, physical therapists, psychiatrists, psychologists, neuropsychologists, developmental pediatricians, learning specialists, etc.); thus, the document can feel dense and overwhelming, albeit necessary as documentation for accommodations. Having one bulleted outline as an appendix can be really helpful.

3. **Recommendations should highlight support and intervention that are necessary at school, as well as outside of school.** The school's learning support team should have a clear understanding of the student's strengths and weaknesses, as should any outside support professionals. Recommendations specific to targeted support should be made; a recommendation should not just be for speech and language therapy, but should also highlight specifically the focus of the necessary intervention (i.e., what that specialist should be working on with a given student depending upon the testing profile).

4. **If outside services are recommended, the clinician should provide referrals and contact information.** These services might include additional tutors, therapies, or medication management.

After all of these years working with my daughter, as well as with so many families of kids with learning challenges, I now understand that I was right to view Melissa's original report with skepticism at first. Psych-ed tests can be your first proactive move toward understanding how your child sees the world and how the teacher sees your child, provided the child has the verbal skills to take the test and is not too intimidated or stressed to try to answer all of the questions. Don't necessarily take the results at face value though. All standardized tests are steeped in the idea of the mythical "average." If parents and educators understand that each child has a jagged learning profile, then the psych-ed report can help them map each child's individual edges, in terms of academic strengths and potential, as compared to their actual performance on subject tests. There are different tests administered to show if potential and achievement are in sync—a large difference between the two can be an indication of a learning difference. If there is a lot of inconsistency in scores showing potential (sometimes referred to as scatter), this can be another indicator of a learning difference.

Proceed With Caution

Most of the tests used by school psychologists and other test administrators are based on a deficit model—that is, they look at the statistical average for children of the same age and place a child's abilities on a scale of comparison to other kids. However, these averages are essentially meaningless in describing an individual's talents and weaknesses.

These tests can, at best, be effective in pointing out a child's weaker areas. Some even have a category on the low end that classifies students as "at risk." How terrifying does that sound? But although these tests are stellar at pointing out shortcomings, they don't necessarily show individual strengths. Understanding a child's strengths can be the key to finding workable pathways to success, so why don't tests look for these strengths instead of just focusing on areas of weakness?

Some forward-thinking psychologists are moving toward a different testing model, one that looks for patterns of strengths *and* weakness. This seems like a win-win for everyone, right? Teachers and specialists would know where students are prone to struggle, but they'd also know where kids naturally shine. Parents would learn how to get kids excited about a topic by employing the right methods to share information. Sadly, relatively few psychologists are trained in this evaluation method. Even in school districts where the school psychologists have received strength and weakness training, the default still may be the traditional deficit-based model. Parents need to ask for the strengths and weakness focus specifically.

In fact, I recommend that all parents include a short note along with the permission slip they are generally asked to sign before a child's evaluation process can begin. The wording here should not be antagonistic or accusatory; you're trying to recruit allies, not alienate people. You could write something along these lines:

> Thank you for starting this evaluation process so we can all work together to help my child succeed at school. If at all possible, we would love it if the evaluation could include some insights into my child's areas of strength and affinity as well as deficits. This could be really helpful to us all as we try to work together to figure out which methods will help my child best. Thanks again! (J. Adams, personal communication, February 2016)

This message is positive and upbeat, and implies that the parent and school staff members are all a team. Ideally, that's what you want: a group of concerned adults, with some experts and some laypeople (and likely some people in between), who are all seeking to support and empower the child in need.

The Tests and Tools

However imperfect, psychoeducational testing is currently a necessary path to the accommodations and services your child will need. More importantly, it can give potential clues that point to the pathways that might be most successful for your child's development. To make these tests helpful for your child, try viewing these tests through a positive lens. No matter what the raw scores are, these tests *will* display trends of strength if you look for them.

When a young child is tested, the process is usually spread out over a few days—it's a lot of material for a little mind! Typically, there are five main areas psychologists test when administering a comprehensive psychoeducational evaluation: background information and history, cognitive functioning, processing ability, academic functioning, and behavior and social-emotional functioning. The end of the report will include a summary of findings, potentially including a diagnosis, and recommendations. Usually, it takes a few weeks to receive the testing report, a lengthy document containing the scores from many different kinds of evaluations. It's not unusual for a child to present very high scores in some areas and very low scores in another (i.e., jaggedness in action).

Be advised that many reports use a combination of different kinds of scores, such as percentiles, raw scores, and normed numbers. Do not be afraid to ask for clarification if any of this is confusing to you. You have the right to understand what information is being imparted about your child.

A parent may be able to notice some things that an evaluator might not: affinities, motivations, knacks. You may have noticed that your child can build, dismantle, and rebuild a LEGO kit in record time when looking at a picture, but might struggle with the same project if reading the directions. You might have noticed that your child remembers the lyrics to a song after hearing it only once but can't read them from a piece of paper with confidence or fluency. Record these observations and add them to your child's report on a separate page—they help to round out the picture of your whole child.

School Accommodations

Depending on what the results indicate, your child's assessment is the gateway to school accommodations. Some parents hesitate at first—*We don't want our child to feel singled out or labeled, do we?*—but if accommodations are used with sensitivity, they can be real game changers. For example, at Melissa's first school, she was always seated at the front of the classroom in an effort to minimize distraction. Although it certainly didn't solve all of her problems, this basic change supported her tremendously. It didn't give her a head start but simply let her start the race at the same time as all of the other kids.

Modern classroom accommodations are evolving—the new push is for *asset-based accommodations*, which go beyond simply reacting to a student's classroom challenges and focus instead on letting them work to their strengths. Instead of writing an essay, a student with dysgraphia might be allowed to create a short film, a slideshow, or an illustration. Instead of watching a short video, a student with receptive language issues might be allowed to read an article about a topic. In both examples, the students are learning key information while also demonstrating subject mastery in a format in which they excel.

Parents of kids who haven't been identified with a learning disability sometimes look at accommodations and think that these kids are getting "special treatment" or "unfair advantages." They might think the kids are being enabled by their parents and teachers. However, enabling is exactly the opposite of what is intended. Instead, these accommodations seek to *empower* kids. Once a student's profile of strengths and weaknesses is mapped, that information can be used to help personalize their education and then help them learn to advocate for themselves, navigating through the world with a clear view of how they learn and what they need for success. Accommodations such as extra time on tests, calculators, and readers level the playing field between neurotypical and neuroatypical brains.

The example of eyeglasses is often used to demonstrate this argument. Not everyone requires eyeglasses, so eyeglasses will not benefit those who don't need them. Studies have proven that extra time on a standardized test does not improve scores for those who do not have a difference in processing speed, for example. In fact, extra time used by a person whose processing speed doesn't require it can cause scores to go down due to second-guessing correct answers (Yale Center for Dyslexia and Creativity, 2017d). On the other hand, I know of many cases where extra time has caused a substantial increase in scores because the person who actually needed it would have otherwise left those questions unanswered.

Reflection

Think about something your child cannot do in the classroom and then jot down some positive interpretations of the behavior. Context can actually change what might be considered bad behavior into positive behavior or a strength in a different setting. For example, a child who is very chatty in school may be considered disruptive, yet in another setting, such as at home or socially, chattiness can be viewed as a people skill or an indication of emotional intelligence.

_____

_____

_____

_____

_____

_____

_____

_____

_____

_____

_____

_____

_____

_____

_____

Part III
A New Way of Thinking

CHAPTER 5

From High School Dropout to Harvard Scientist

When I first met Todd Rose at a conference in 2013, he was a young professor of neuroscience at Harvard's Graduate School of Education. I was immediately drawn to his fresh viewpoint on the capabilities of people with learning challenges. Rose (2013) grew up in a small town in Utah, had trouble fitting in at his mainstream school, and eventually dropped out of high school. But through hard work, an understanding of his own strengths, and some luck, he ended up on the faculty at Harvard.

Rose spent his academic career focusing on finding a way to talk about individual differences without buying into the idea that they are disabilities. His term of choice when I first met him was "variability" (Rose, 2013), which he argued was normal and natural from a scientific viewpoint in the human population.

From there, Rose (2016) studied the ways in which schools and the education system at large were originally designed to train workers to man the factories and burgeoning bureaucracies created by the Industrial Revolution in the early 19th century, using a theoretical "average student" template that did not actually exist. Rose used neuroscientific data to prove that variability is, in fact, the norm, and that the outdated education system—founded in the dehumanizing days of the Industrial Revolution—

has created millions of "square peg" kids who are intelligent, capable, and motivated but not served by their mainstream schools.

I was impressed with Rose's resilience and brilliance, as well as his message: With a strong support network and a good work ethic, the square pegs of the world can go on to do incredible things. His first book, *Square Peg: My Story and What It Means for Raising Innovators, Visionaries, and Out-of-the-Box Thinkers*, was a beacon of hope and a manifesto for many parents who knew that their kids, despite being misfits at school, were smart, strong, and capable, but had not yet found a way to scholastic success (Rose, 2013).

But what came next excited me even more. Rose (2016) applied his neuroscience knowledge, his intensive educational research, and observations from his own personal journey to help develop the science of individuality and to apply its principles to learning and performance for all. Although these theories are applicable to everyone, I was struck by the potential they have to vastly improve education for students who learn differently. Understanding what Rose calls the "Science of Individuality," which encourages people to embrace and encourage each individual's inherent complexity, can be an important early step for parents of kids with learning challenges as they move to help their nontypical children succeed in a world designed to reward sameness.

Accepting this shift in focus, from fixing kids' flaws to helping them develop their strengths, is the first step in the process of what I call "Parenting Reframed." In my case, this meant looking for ways in which my daughter's prodigious talents could be engaged while I helped her study. Knowing that movement helped her focus, I typed her impressive summary of a book report while she rollerbladed and dictated aloud, accommodating for her writing struggles and encouraging her verbal strengths.

I also started treating her with teen magazines because she read them cover to cover and became full of information in conversations with her friends. My parenting became more effective and fun when I focused on her strengths and how to help her develop a strong sense of her own abilities. It was too easy for her (and for me) to lose sight of all her natural talents, while every day she would face different situations that highlighted her unease with fluent reading, spelling, recognizing unfamiliar words, and math facts. I had started focusing on strengths as I mimicked what I saw the teachers doing at the Charles Armstrong School.

After listening to a few presentations by Rose, I realized he was giving words to a process I was already learning how to do. When I heard him draw together the cutting-edge research from many fields into the Science of Individuality, I clearly saw the application to parenting (Rose, 2016). Using his three key concepts—what he termed a "jagged profile," the importance of context, and multiple pathways—to adjust the lens through which I viewed the abilities and potential of not only my daughter, but also others around me, helped me develop more positive and effective relationships with family and friends.

The Science of Individuality

In *The End of Average: How We Succeed in a World That Values Sameness*, Rose (2016) laid out a new way of thinking about success in his Science of Individuality. He first dismantled the idea that "average" is a meaningful yardstick for measuring performance. He offered the example of U.S. Air Force fighter pilots, who were not performing as well as they were expected to in the 1950s. After some study, the Air Force realized that the cockpits of the planes were based on the measurements of the average fighter pilot. But on further examination, it was established that there was no such thing as an average fighter pilot; each pilot had unique dimensions—arm length, torso height, weight, and body length from foot to shoulder. This meant that the cockpit designed to fit the average pilot actually fit no one.

There is, essentially, no such thing as an average human, either physically, mentally, or behaviorally. So why are so many tools (like standardized tests) based on averages? Why are schools and textbooks based on age-appropriate averages and methods that may work for the average student?

Rose (2016) argued that people must abandon the idea of average in schools, work, and life, just as they have abandoned the concept in the field of medicine. Personalized medicine, which takes into account every aspect of a patient's physical well-being, from the bacteria in the gut to the nuances of one's genetic makeup, is revolutionizing healthcare right now and offering people far better outcomes than the one-size-fits-all approach of yesterday.

To maximize the talent in our world, people must embrace and encourage each individual's inherent complexity. That, in essence, is the Science of Individuality.

Jaggedness, Context, and Pathways

Rose's (2016) theory is based on three main tenets: jaggedness, context, and pathways (or trajectories).

Jaggedness

Each individual person is made up of edges, with a jagged profile of strengths and weaknesses (Rose, 2016). No two people have an identical intellectual profile, and no two people have the exact same mix of talents, affinities, and deficits. For example, I'm great at reading people and having lively conversations, but not at remembering names. I've always known this about myself, but Rose gave me a vocabulary for it. Every person has individual high and low "edges." Each student has their own jagged profile, and each learning profile has its own topography. (Refer to Figure 2 on p. 50 for an example of a jagged profile.)

Context

Another grounding principle is the notion of context. How people perform is not just dependent on jaggedness and the pathway they are using, but also on the context surrounding them (Rose, 2016).

Standardized tests are a great example. There's a reason why students are instructed to get a good night's sleep and have a healthy breakfast the night before the SAT; having basic physical needs met can help performance. But what if a student has a history of subpar performance on tests? Nerves and anxiety could mushroom into full-blown panic. The context of the standardized test setting could have a negative impact on the student's ability to recall things that they actually know.

Another example is learning multiplication tables. Students can sit down and drill if that works for their brains. Or they can strap on a pair of roller skates and glide around the room chanting the answers, as my daughter Melissa did. She was a very physical kid, always in motion, and using her body helped her to embed knowledge into her consciousness. The movement on skates helped her to remember the answers. That was the context she needed to get to the same result as the kids who drilled. The context that works for some may not necessarily work for others. Moreover, finding the right context is relevant to specific activities. For example, a baseball pitcher often finds his favorite field, one whose size and angles allows him to play at his best; many excellent public speakers have their favorite audience size and type. Everyone needs to identify what works for them and follow that method. The end result matters, not the tool used to get there.

Pathways

Additionally, Rose (2016) introduced the concept of multiple trajectories, or pathways, to end with the same result. There is more than one way to become a faculty member at Harvard, as he has proven. Some take the expected path—excelling in high school, attending a prestigious college, and scoring a plum fellowship before being hired into the Ivy League. Their strengths match those valued by the current educational system; the well-trod pathway works for them.

But brilliant minds learn in many different ways, and some of these modes did not fit into traditional classrooms until very recently. The pathways these students might take to success could look very different. It's a matter of finding what works for each child—what helps them to perform best and realize their potential. Perhaps the best two examples of different pathways are illustrated by the careers of Steve Jobs and Bill Gates. Both were college dropouts, and through very different but somewhat unconventional career paths at the time—risky start-ups—both founded iconic, successful businesses that made a huge mark on the tech industry. Biographies of both men reveal somewhat quirky personalities and out-of-the-box thinking as common themes.

Understanding these dimensions and traits is the key to effectively parenting and supporting a child with learning differences. If Rose's ideas had been on my radar when Melissa was first diagnosed, I might have been spared years of worry, stress, and anxiety. Understanding that her jagged profile was such a mismatch with a girls' private school in San Francisco, I would have felt no compunction about changing her school and her context as soon as she began to fail. As it was, I agonized over this decision, which cost her a lot of time in the process of learning how to learn.

With a growth-based mindset and a solid belief in variability, I would have been comfortable taking Melissa out of her kindergarten class right away. I could have found a more developmental way to introduce her to the academics that would prove to be so difficult for her to master, thus avoiding the dragged-out "drowning in deficits" years in elementary school when her plummeting self-esteem caused her to morph into a different child.

I maybe would have asked her more often to tell me what she *wanted* to do instead of trying to direct her into what I saw as her strengths.

Variability, Not Disability

Once I grasped the basic ideas of the Science of Individuality, I couldn't accept the notion that a learning difference is a valid way to categorize a student. Yes, there are strategies that help students with dyslexia read or help those with attention challenges learn to focus. But defining a student with this type of label is not only misleading, but also self-defeating. Educators and parents have missed so much talent and so many opportunities by pigeonholing kids. They have willfully ignored jaggedness, performance in context, and alternative pathways, and have done many millions of people a disservice, not to mention deprived society of sorely needed talent.

One of the real problems arising from the use of a disability model and the negative language that comes with it is the constant focus on fixing what's wrong instead of looking at all of the things that are right and exciting about children. Parents run the risk of getting caught up in the "Negative Tetris Effect," a phenomenon that Shawn Achor (2010) referred to in his book *The Happiness Advantage*. Achor defined the Negative Tetris Effect as "a cognitive pattern resulting from too much practice in looking at the negative instead of the positive" (p. 93). My daughter's story clearly demonstrates the unhappy results that come from focusing too intently on the negative while ignoring the positive.

All kids want to learn. Understanding this, and figuring out how to facilitate that learning, is the only way to help kids contribute in their own individual ways. Once this thinking sinks in, it's impossible to go back to the old disability model. The generalized, one-dimensional way of defining a kid's learning potential is simply incorrect and unscientific.

Reflection

Reflect for a minute on your close friends and acquaintances. Is there an example of unconventionality or a surprise success among them? What about you? Were there some instances in your own life when you chose a surprising or unconventional pathway to a certain goal? Did your early life predict what you might become in later life?

Now think about your child. What are some different pathways you might suggest to your child for finding future satisfaction, using their jagged profile and the contexts in which their strengths come to the fore?

_____

_____

_____

_____

_____

_____

_____

_____

_____

_____

_____

_____

_____

_____

CHAPTER 6

Jaggedness
The Norm, Not the Exception

Once your eyes have been opened to the diversity of learning styles, processing methods, and inherent traits in humanity, you'll never stop seeing it. Over the years, whether I was working with my daughter on her homework, talking with a fellow parent who wanted to be involved with PEN, collaborating with educators and psychologists to plan events, or simply making my way through our social community, I couldn't stop noticing how different everyone's skill sets and abilities were and the impact that context has on effectiveness.

Some children are lucky enough to perform well in the areas that traditional schooling values: verbal processing, receptive language, and executive function. But for those kids whose jagged edges don't line up with the most common methods used in mainstream education, a certain amount of self-reflection, lens shifting, and creativity is needed in order to maximize potential and succeed.

The jaggedness principle laid out in Rose's (2016) Science of Individuality theory makes it clear that one-dimensional thinking is insufficient to understand something as complex as an individual's neurological makeup. The jaggedness principle demands that educators and parents look at each student's—indeed, each person's—neural profile as a set of strengths and weaknesses, all roughly related to each other, but each to a different degree and subject to change in different contexts.

Not every person has such dramatic differences in their areas of strength and challenge, but for each and every child, those peaks and valleys are there; the bigger the spread of abilities, the worse the fit into a particular school culture is likely to be, and the greater the judgments from peers. The secret to helping these children succeed is figuring out how to utilize their strengths to work around their weaknesses. I call this "being aware of your edges," or "teaching and parenting to the edges."

Your Child Is Not You

Just as every kid has their own jagged profile, so does each parent. Think about your edges: You know your highs, and you're painfully aware of your lows. If you think about it, you can probably even jot down some ways that you use your higher edges to compensate when faced with tasks that call on your lower edge skills.

Your jagged profile may not match up with your child's; if you were to lay a graph of your profile over your child's, the peaks and valleys could be totally reversed. That can be hard, and even painful, to try to understand.

For example, a friend of mine was an extremely early reader. She read spontaneously at age 3, was bumped up to upper-grade classrooms for reading all throughout elementary school, and eventually went on to win prizes and accolades for her writing skills. She majored in English and studied at the most prestigious graduate creative writing program in the country, the University of Iowa.

When her daughter was born, my friend filled her child's nursery with books. She fantasized about sharing her favorite novels with her daughter, and then swapping books back and forth when her daughter became an adult. She read aloud to her young daughter constantly and waited patiently for her to spontaneously learn to read—the way that my friend had.

But her daughter had other plans. When she started preschool, she showed very little interest in reading. Throughout kindergarten and first grade, she resisted learning to read and refused to practice with her mother at home. By second grade, she was a whole grade level behind in her literacy skills, struggling through texts that her classmates had breezed through in kindergarten. Even as her fluency gradually began to improve, she hated to read at home. "Reading is boring!" she proclaimed. If she was forced to read something, she preferred books of facts, like Guinness World Records.

My friend was completely flummoxed. She had spent most of her childhood wrapped up in fictional worlds, absorbing novels. How could a child ever hope to "get lost" in Guinness World Records? She tried not to show her child the emotions she felt about her lack of literacy: anxiety, sadness, disappointment, fear. Friends would try to reassure her: "Don't worry, it will come in time—soon you won't be able to get her nose out of a book." But my friend suspected that a love of reading just wasn't in her daughter's makeup; she wasn't that kid.

Her daughter exhibited some focus and organization problems in the classroom, and has since been labeled with ADHD. The label has helped her teacher to strategize and use her strengths, such as movement, creativity, and art, to help her focus in class.

Recently, my friend discovered the Science of Individuality and began to look for her daughter's jaggedness. Yes, reading is a lower edge for her daughter, but she has higher edges in visual and auditory processing. She loves to draw, loves music, and loves to act out dramatically. My friend began to look for ways to use these aptitudes and affinities to help her child access the imaginative world. She collaborated with her daughter to make books, writing stories that her daughter illustrated. She enrolled her daughter in piano lessons, which her daughter loved. She got her daughter involved with a theater school where her daughter could engage with narratives in a dramatic way.

Another good example of how misleading it can be to focus on low edges without considering high edges is that of a young boy I'll call Roy. His diagnosis of dyslexia had caused his mother to research a new method of training the ear for phoneme recognition, called Fast Forward. This program, developed at University of California-San Francisco, got a lot of attention when it was first developed in the 1990s. A child would use a computer program to practice sounds with letter recognition. Clinical trials had shown impressive results from use of the program and increases in reading fluency.

Roy found the program very boring, and his distractibility caused him to miss a lot of the cues. But his mother continued to have him work at home with the program. In his downtime, Roy would read car magazines, even staying up every night past his bedtime reading under the covers with a flashlight. When he was caught doing this, he was usually punished by having his car magazines taken away. Finally, Roy's reading tutor convinced Roy's mother that Fast Forward could be cancelled, and more time given to Roy during the day to read his car magazines. The freedom to read what interested him motivated Roy to practice and improve his reading skills. Interests lead to strengths, and passion in an area of interest leads to greater proficiency.

By devoting time to understanding their child's jagged profile of highs and lows, parents can promote the development and use of strengths to compensate for weaknesses. New science in the field of positive psychology focuses on systematically identifying and helping your child identify strengths. When figuring out your child's jagged profile, look for strengths as they are defined in the book *The Strength Switch* (Waters, 2017). In short, the book explains that learning to accept and celebrate your child as an individual, not as an extension of yourself, is one of the great challenges—and great gifts—of parenthood.

When trying to establish your child's profile, remember that they are not you or your spouse, or even a recognizable combination of their parents. Each individual is as unique as a fingerprint. In addition, if you and your spouse did well in school (or, at least, you remember doing well), it may be impossible for you to truly understand what your child is experiencing. Therefore, it may be particularly difficult to develop the empathy you will need to support them in their academic struggles. In cases like this, the development of a jagged profile might seem more like an academic exercise. Hiring a tutor who is trained to teach those who learn differently may get better results with your child. Another benefit of hiring an outside trained tutor is the preservation of a less stressful relationship with your child.

Acknowledging that there are many different pathways to learning is the next step to truly maximizing your child's success. Parenting to your child's edges—maximizing the highs and minimizing the lows—is the best way to help your child own those edges as an adult.

A SIDENOTE ON TUTORING

Keep in mind that the single most important factor in supporting a child's success is a nurturing adult who is there, unconditionally, to support the student, no matter what. Parents often want to fill this role, but it is hard for them to do this properly. Parents love their children unconditionally but bring a lot of baggage to the relationship: expectations (unspoken or verbalized), guilt, and regret. It's also common for parents of children with learning issues, ADHD in particular, to realize along the way that they themselves are afflicted with the same disorder as their children. This was certainly my case; as I began to delve into the theories and diagnostics for my daughter, I realized I displayed many of the characteristics of a person with ADHD. Further tests confirmed that diagnosis, launching me on my own illuminating voyage of self-discovery.

Seeing a child struggle academically or socially can bring back painful memories for parents, which can get in the way of unconditional support for the child. Often, a person outside of the parent/child dyad is the most effective support person. Partly, this is because children *expect* support and love from their own parents; when a person outside of that dichotomy offers unconditional support, children value and invest in that relationship even more.

Establishing Your Child's Jagged Profile

The principle that everyone has their own individual jagged profile is perhaps the most significant piece of information parents need in order to accept their child's differences. By definition, this principle implies that jaggedness is normal and that every child has strengths as well as challenges—even if those strengths are not obvious in a school setting.

Schools, with their focus on grades that span the entire academic spectrum, often presuppose that children should be skilled equally in all academic subjects. If they are not, students are sometimes perceived as being lazy. This limited thinking is a product of the psychologists of the 1960s. Abilities were thought to be the same and predictable across domains. For example, if someone was gifted academically, that person was thought to be able to perform in all academic subjects equally well—and beyond that in other areas, like athletics, music, art, etc.

But the idea of the jagged profile suggests a different way for parents to know their child: by figuring out the child's strengths and weaknesses. For example, in *The End of Average*, Rose (2016) pointed out that two students with the same IQ might have vastly different jagged profiles (p. 89).

Suppose both girls explain a concept on a paper. If the girl with the much better vocabulary uses more accurate wording but has a less clear understanding of the concept, her writing skills could hide her lack of knowledge on the topic. Likewise, the girl with a firmer grasp of the concept but a weaker writing style might be hiding her conceptual strength with her weaker vocabulary.

Some teachers accommodate this difference on an individual basis by assigning different grades to content and presentation. This type of individualized grading requires knowing each student's particular strengths and weaknesses, and is a much better way to motivate bright students who have trouble showing what they know. Explaining your child's jagged profile can be a wonderful way to ask a teacher to give your child separate grades for handwriting (if it is poor) and for ideas (which may be very creative), or for subject matter that must be mastered.

Standardized school reports for a child who is, for example, dyslexic can be problematic because the child's academic strengths will most likely seem low, as reading is the foundation for most standardized tests. But the child's creativity in thinking and art, organizational and other executive function skills, and high degree of athleticism and athletic intelligence could also lead them to an interest in sports, advertising, or architecture. My husband and I encouraged all of those fields in Melissa whenever and however we could. A child's visual skills may be off the charts, but unfortunately, they are not included in standard curricula.

When Melissa started working in the various sections of the family's real estate business as an adult, she was exposed to the skills of building or renovating houses for resale. Her risk-taking, ability to manage a team, aesthetic appreciation of construction features and neighborhoods, and need for daily novel tasks were a great fit for that side of the business. She now has her own development business and tells me that her dyslexia and discomfort with math are no longer issues for her, as she always works in a team with others who have compensating skills.

Understanding your child's jagged profile will allow you to individualize their learning, so you can break down material and tasks into the pieces that they like and those that they still need to work on. Monthly report cards and teacher comments, along with your child's own version of these evaluations, will help develop a 360-degree view of your child. Your child's input is also valuable in finding out how easy or difficult these tasks are for them and why—a big piece of the learning puzzle.

Another way to get insight into your child's strengths and weaknesses is to play games together. Some people are born strategists, while others are more interested in playing by the conventional rules. Board games can be very helpful in showing strengths like interpersonal skills when taking turns and handling competition, as well as observing certain skill sets. For example, with simple matching games, such as Memory, it is easy to see how observant a child is and if visual memory is a strength. For older kids, a game like Monopoly shows strategic thinking, talent with counting, and money sorting.

Knowing your child's jagged profile gives you an opportunity to visualize with your child what kind of work would really interest them and give them joy and energy. Taking a long view of your child's strengths can also relieve the pressure of any low performance you may be witnessing right now and allow instead for dreams and passions to form.

"These are great drawings of different kinds of houses," you might tell your child. "Maybe you will want to be a builder of houses, an architect who designs houses, or a decorator who designs the interiors of houses. Or, with your people skills and business sense, maybe you will be a seller of houses. You have lots of choices ahead of you, and you will thrive with your strengths and avoid work that is boring or difficult for you."

The ultimate goal of understanding your child's jagged profile is to teach them how to understand themselves—their best tool for taking charge of their education and future. In my experience, kids are more aware than you may think of what they are good at and where their struggles lie. Talking with and interacting with your child remains one of the best ways to empower them to take charge, as soon as they are ready.

Reflection

Take a minute to write down what some of your own jagged edges might be, including highs and lows. Then write down some of your child's obvious jagged edges. For example:

- Low edge: I am a fluent reader, who is very comfortable reading aloud. My child is not fluent when she reads aloud.
- High edge: I find it hard to grasp and remember key points and concepts from listening to others read aloud. My child understands key points and concepts when she listens to others read aloud.

_____

_____

_____

_____

_____

_____

_____

_____

_____

_____

_____

_____

_____

_____

CHAPTER 7

Context
The Key to Unlocking Talent

The first time the head of the Charles Armstrong School phoned me, I was nervous. I wondered, *What has gone wrong now?* My family had been through so much; I just wanted a few months without a panicked phone call from the school office.

"I'm just calling to let you how well things are going," Dr. W said warmly. Four years' worth of pain, worry, and suffering left my strained shoulders.

When Melissa started at her new school, where all of the children were dyslexic and the teaching was focused on learning to read proficiently, her reading scores began to improve almost immediately. She became less anxious and defensive—a welcome change from her attitude at her previous school, where she was in constant fight-or-flight mode. Being under the care of supportive adults and studying alongside so many kids who had experienced similar struggles did wonders for her. She calmed down enough to be able to learn again. At home, where she was safest, she easily settled down at the dining room table to do her homework, practicing recognizing words on sight and reading aloud. Homework time quickly became less of a struggle and more of a bonding time. I began to look forward to it rather than dread it.

Still, even with these positive changes, I noticed that Melissa got agitated, even paralyzed, when multiple sequential directions were fed to her too quickly at home or at school. However, out on the soccer field, where she was one of the best players, this wasn't an issue. No matter how fast the coach shouted multistep directions, like "get over to the center, kick the ball to Sarah, and stay in the middle," Melissa seemed to have no trouble following his sequence of commands.

Lessons about context were all around me. Melissa was thriving at her new school because it was the right context for her. There, she was set up to achieve academic success. And in the context of a fast-moving soccer game, she was able to perform differently than in a classroom. I would soon learn that it had been foolish of me to expect Melissa to perform consistently across all situations, because *no one* is consistent across all situations. Context affects us all.

Context Affects Performance

Context is a key concept of the Science of Individuality; a person's surroundings and environment inevitably affect their behavior. No two people will perform identically in the same context, because each person brings their own unique combination of jagged edges and pathway experience into each situation. Performance in one context isn't always indicative of ability. In looking for strengths and weaknesses, context can change things dramatically. For example, my husband and I believed that an all-girls school would encourage our daughters to be more outgoing—with the idea that boys can be distracting for self-conscious girls and intimidating enough to inhibit effort and risk-taking academically. This turned out to be the best decision for our very studious and compliant older daughter, but not so much for Melissa, who felt more comfortable with boisterous boys than with quiet, nonactive, studious girls.

Certain contexts work better for some people than others. Think about yourself: Maybe you are willing to take big risks in an active context, like rock climbing or river rafting, but you are extremely cautious and conservative when it comes to your finances. Maybe you're loud and boisterous with your friends from high school, but quiet and reserved with your coworkers. That's all context.

My own work history is an excellent example of the power of context. I was not the kind of person who could just take any job and do well. In the 16 years from college graduation until I got married, I was constantly looking for the perfect job. I was vaguely aware that a normal office environment—where I was expected to sit still and work at a desk by myself—was not a comfortable fit for me. But because I didn't fully understand my strengths and weaknesses, I made some disastrous mistakes in job selection during those years.

The very worst fit for my personality and talents was at an international consulting firm, where I worked as a librarian in the research department. There, I had to face my ineptitudes daily. Keeping records of reorders for annual publications was particularly difficult. More than once, I was asked for the latest edition of a periodical, only to realize with embarrassment that I had no idea if I had even ordered it.

My office was a very small library on the 51st floor of a posh building in downtown San Francisco. My desk was right in front of the stacks of books out in the hallway, so people could see me. This was the worst possible place for me to get any work done, due to my distractible nature. I always had a crowd of people around me trading jokes and stories. After about a year, I moved my desk into a corner so I could concentrate. This worked for a while until I realized that I could happily talk on the phone for hours with no one noticing. It's amazing that I lasted there for 4 years!

My best job—one that seemed practically designed for me—was as a merchandiser at Levi Strauss & Co. I worked on jeans, including the world-famous 501, the company's most popular brand. Although the location of my desk was still open to distractions, the work actually demanded a lot of social interaction as well as information analysis. I was deeply interested in the business aspects of how best to make a profit for the company. Armed with the tools I had learned at business school, I was excited to go to work every day and make my contribution. Making an active minute-by-minute and day-by-day contribution kept my focus sharp.

Rose's (2013) own story illustrates the power of context. At school, he was often disruptive. He was constantly being suspended and reprimanded for his behavior. But at home, with his grandmother, he was a different person—calmer, more reasonable, and able to control his impulsive behavior, which might upset his grandmother. School was a place of tension and fear for him, and he acted accordingly. But with his grandmother, he was safe and didn't feel the need to act out.

Creating a Context for Success at Home

After discovering more about learning differences, I realized how unsafe our home must have felt for Melissa. In the beginning, I was still trying to get her to behave without understanding why she was so out of control. For kids who learn differently, home should feel like a safe haven after an often-unfriendly school day. Before observing this myself, I had not embraced the idea of this necessity for safety. Only when I saw my own child feeling comfortable taking risks in a safe academic space did I begin to fully appreciate this.

Bob Brooks, a world-renowned psychologist who has lectured extensively and authored many books on parenting kids with learning differences, has written about developing a safe and supportive context for children to learn in, both at home and in the classroom. Creating a safe environment at home, a space for kids to be who they really are and celebrate their differences, goes beyond making sure they are physically safe. They must also feel psychologically and emotionally safe. This type of context is the place where a child can perform best.

Brooks (2014) pointed to resilience—the ability to bounce back after adversity—as one of the key traits to nurture in children. With resilience, kids can do well even when placed in contexts that challenge them. Brooks identified the mindset of resilient children this way:

> They feel special and appreciated.
>
> They have learned to set realistic goals and expectations for themselves.
>
> They believe that they have the ability to solve problems and make sound decisions and thus are more likely to view mistakes, setbacks, and obstacles as challenges to confront rather than as stressors to avoid.
>
> They rely on effective coping strategies that promote growth and are not self-defeating.
>
> They are aware of and do not deny their weaknesses and vulnerabilities but view them as areas for improvement rather than as unchangeable flaws.
>
> They recognize and enjoy their strong points and talents.

Their self-concept is filled with images of strength and competence.

They feel comfortable with others and have developed effective interpersonal skills with peers and adults alike. This enables them to seek out assistance and nurturance in a comfortable, appropriate manner from adults who can provide the support they need.

They are able to define the aspects of their lives over which they have control and to focus their energy and attention on these, rather than on factors over which they have little, or any, influence. (p. 446)

So how can parents nurture resilient children at home? What goes into this type of mindset and attitude? Brooks (2014) included the following advice for parents:

- **Be empathic:** Try to put yourself in your child's shoes.
- **Communicate effectively and listen actively:** Try to really understand what your child is saying.
- **Change negative scripts:** If an approach is not working with your child, don't use it anymore.
- **Love children in ways that make them feel special and appreciated:** Let your child know that you believe in them and love them unconditionally.
- **Accept children for who they are and help them to establish realistic expectation and goals:** Try to understand and honor their talents and temperaments.
- **Help children experience success by identifying and nurturing their "islands of competence":** Brooks referred to high edges (i.e., strengths) as islands of competence, or a child's areas of expertise.
- **Help children realize that mistakes are experiences from which to learn:** Detach shame and blame from failure, emphasizing the lessons of each mistake.
- **Develop responsibility, compassion, and social conscience by providing children with opportunities to contribute:** Meaningful social projects enhance feelings of efficacy and usefulness.
- **Discipline in ways that promote self-discipline and self-worth:** Be mindful of the child's experience of the discipline.

- **Choose your battlegrounds:** Not everything is worth a confrontation.
- **Rely on natural and logical consequences:** Let the experience guide the child.
- **Provide positive feedback and encouragement:** Targeted praise is the basis of solid parenting.

Home must be a haven, especially for kids who feel powerless at school. Had I had these reminders about creating a safe space at home when I was going through the hardest years of parenting my daughter, I would have taped the list to my mirror and looked at it constantly.

When things are falling apart at school, it is more important than ever to establish a safe, supportive haven at home. If children are struggling with a teacher who doesn't "get" them or peers who are less-than-understanding of their challenges, then parents at home should avoid adding to that pressure. It can be difficult for parents to focus on unconditional love and ignore the academic stress when children exhibit behavior that seems self-sabotaging. However, many psychologists say that this is the best thing parents can do for struggling kids.

Giving Melissa her own path to follow without my guidance was the hardest thing for me to do. College was a particularly difficult time for me to let go of the scaffolding I'd been providing. Over the years, Melissa had the opportunity to emphatically remind me to "butt out of her life" several times, and it took a while for me to get the message. Once, she asked me to come to the UC Berkeley with her to meet the resource director and help her spend the day getting comfortable on campus. I was very excited about doing this with her, and even more thrilled that she had invited me to come along.

It didn't take long for our visit to change from exciting to excruciating. I started to feel anxiety creeping up, and although I tried to hide it, Melissa soon caught on. When she asked me what was wrong, I shared my story of attending the University of Florida, a similar school in many ways, and how uncomfortable I was when I was there: the huge campus, the crush of so many people around all of the time, the impersonal relationships between faculty and students. I was just a number at Florida, and I worried that it would be the same way for her.

She was quick to explain to me that she wasn't applying to this school as a normal student but had been invited by the coach of the rowing team, an affirmation of her high athletic skill and dedication to this sport.

Already, her experience was different; she would have a ready-made community and support system. I listened. She had learned what she needed, and she could recognize when she was getting it.

The first year of college, she agreed that her grades could be viewed by her parents. By her sophomore year, she rescinded that privilege. "Mom, I'm in charge of my own education now," she said.

She was right, and I knew it.

When I finally learned to sit back and stop my "helpful" interfering, it improved both our relationship and her confidence. I know now that when your child asks you to back off, you probably should—it is vital for their empowerment that they have their own successes and failures.

A change in context can mean everything to a child. After hearing me speak at a conference, a friend of mine approached me in tears. Her son had been struggling, exhibiting strange behavior at school. "He's gotten so weird," she cried. (Later, I learned that he had been diagnosed with Asperger's, but she couldn't bring herself to say the word yet.) Although her son wasn't actually dyslexic, I suspected that the staff at the Charles Armstrong School could help him. The strength-based curriculum and the supportive community had done such wonders for Melissa that I thought it would be worth it to try. I spoke to the head of school, unsure whether it would be a good fit for this child.

"We won't know until he gets here, really," the head of the school said. "He's covering up so much pain and discomfort at his current school—he may behave totally differently here." So, my friend's son moved to CAS and, lo and behold, he began to thrive. In this environment, his innate intelligence could shine. His teachers worked with his quirks, not against them. The new context was exactly what he needed.

Context is at work in everything our kids do. At CAS, the sympathetic and understanding teachers themselves became the context in which Melissa and others thrived. Parents have the responsibility—and the privilege—of making the home a safe and positive place for their kids.

Reflection

Think about a trait you have noticed in your child that changes in different contexts. For example, do they act differently around other parents than they do around you? Do they perform some tasks well when they think that no one is watching and then perform differently in front of others? How do they perform in sports versus school?

_____

_____

_____

_____

_____

_____

_____

_____

_____

_____

_____

_____

_____

_____

CHAPTER 8

Pathways
Always More Than One

Pathways are funny things. Perhaps you set out on a trail you assume will be flat and easy, and it turns out to be a near-vertical climb. Or you gear yourself up for a grueling trek, only to discover a shortcut that leads you quickly to the finish. Sometimes, your pathway leads you someplace totally unexpected.

Pathways show that there is *always* more than one way to a goal or a learning concept. This is not only common sense, but also one of the main principles of the Science of Individuality (Rose, 2016). The basic principle of pathways—the idea that multiple methods, techniques, or trajectories can eventually lead to the same outcome—proves that, with patience and perseverance, every child can find a route to success.

When parents first hear the diagnosis of their child's learning issues—when the quirks they have noticed are suddenly labeled as *dyslexia* or *ADHD*—it too often sounds and feels like a diagnosis of a disease. What's more, this labeling often signals to parents that there are major limitations to their child's potential for achievement, as though a neurological difference is an immovable obstacle.

A positive parenting approach must embrace the concept of pathways. When parents are already thinking about pathways, they will instinctively encourage a child who is struggling with reading, writing, or learning a new concept to try a different approach. Parents can enable children to know themselves as learners and advocate for themselves to maximize potential.

For example, dyslexia is a label used to describe difficulty with all aspects of language, from receiving to expressing. There are now many different programs, curricula, and apps available to teachers for teaching reading and writing to children with dyslexia in alternative ways from what is typically used in a classroom. Most adults with dyslexia can receive information and express themselves in multiple ways, depending on their own jagged profiles. They could be auditory learners, or better able to absorb concepts visually. Many adults with learning challenges understand what works for them and what doesn't, even when they don't necessarily identify this as a pathway to learning.

Temple Grandin: The Magic of the Right Path

During the years of my ongoing self-education, I had the opportunity to meet and hear Temple Grandin (2015) speak about her autism. Grandin is well known for her study of animal behavior and the revolutionary designs she has produced for more humane and effective agriculture practices. In her books, she eloquently described the various ways her mother advocated to make sure she was getting the accommodations she needed. She herself now advocates for accommodations in order to help people with autism succeed, both academically and professionally.

Unapologetic about her lack of mainstream social graces, Grandin knows what she needs from others, and isn't afraid to ask for it. When someone asks her a theoretical question, she almost shouts, "I need specifics—I don't deal in abstracts!" The inquirer is often a little taken aback by this bluntness, but Grandin goes on to ask the speaker to rephrase the question in very specific terms, so that she can then extrapolate the more universal answer.

Grandin's mother, an intelligent woman far ahead of her time, listened to her own instincts about her different daughter. She refused to accept a diagnosis of "brain damage," which was what doctors settled on around the time Grandin was 2 in the late 1940s. It was recommended that the

Grandins institutionalize their daughter, but Temple's mother rejected this plan. Through trial and error, Grandin's mother finally settled on a pathway that could help her daughter to thrive: She sent her daughter to her sister's farm (Jackson, 2010). At the farm, young Grandin could connect with animals, which was comforting, intriguing, and exciting for her. There, she found her specific passion and talent for industrial design and agriculture.

Today, Grandin is the foremost expert on handling and managing livestock in the world. Her insights into animal behavior have revolutionized farming and slaughterhouse practices, and she has invented machinery that is considered state-of-the-art internationally. She teaches and speaks, not just about animal behavior, but about the differences in the way she experiences the world. In 2010, she was included in *Time* magazine's 100 most influential people in the world.

Grandin's forward-thinking mother allowed her to follow a nontraditional pathway, rejecting the conventional thinking of the time that specified that her daughter would never amount to anything. The right pathway—one informed by farming—brought out the brilliance in this differently-thinking woman.

A Change of Pace

Many factors can affect a child's ability to perform at school, but one of the most important is pace.

When Melissa started seventh grade, she took a beginning algebra class that had been separated into two groups. The groups would learn concepts at different paces. Up until this time, I had been told that her math skills were below grade level. This was hard for my husband to understand because when he worked with her at night, hunched over word problems and pages of equations, he would often say how impressed he was with her reasoning skills. When Melissa was placed in the slower paced group with a teacher who was very patient and relaxed in her teaching, she became much more confident in her math abilities. Slowly and gradually, Melissa began to thrive in math class.

Quite literally, a change of pace was all she needed. Over the course of that year and the next, she was able take in new concepts at her own pace.

The teacher made math class a much safer environment for her, and she was able to learn effectively.

Art as a History Lesson

My friend Megan's daughter, Penelope, has a hard time retaining information gleaned from books—the traditional pathway for subjects like history—but she loves art. Her mother figured out that if she took Penelope to art museums, she could open up a conversation about history by talking with Penelope about what was going on in the world when particular works were painted.

Penelope retains even more information when she creates her own art depicting historical events. She can focus intently for hours, soaking up facts, adding details, and most importantly, learning about the past. Megan realized that Penelope is an experiential learner, a student who needs to use her hands and create something in order to remember. Penelope needs a visual element to her learning, too. When these pieces are present, Penelope becomes an engaged, accomplished student.

This discovery was fascinating to Megan, who has always been a verbal/linguistic learner. School was always easy for her, because her learning style was word-heavy; she loved to read, could retain information from books effortlessly, and took narrative notes to help her remember things. Luckily for Megan, these were the traditional pathways used in schools for many years. It was confusing and distressing for her when she saw that her daughter didn't learn well this way, because this mode of learning had worked for her and was the sanctioned mode of the schools.

As Penelope advances in school, she is learning to advocate for herself. In class, she often draws pictures instead of writing narrative notes and tells her teacher that the drawings help her learn. More traditional teachers might interpret this strategy as goofing off, but they must look with a new lens: Penelope is using a different pathway, one that works better for her. Each child has these inroads, if a patient parent, teacher, or other adult is willing to work with them.

The Path for My Daughter

Rowing crew cleared the path to college for Melissa. My sister was a high school counselor at the time Melissa was looking at colleges, and she passed on multiple lists of small, Division III schools with rowing teams. To my dismay, Melissa tore the lists up. She told me she was already talking to several rowing coaches who had been reaching out to her. Princeton was one of the schools, as well as UC Berkeley, much to my surprise and pleasure. When she told me that she had talked to the Princeton coach about her dyslexia and that together they decided UC Berkeley was a better choice for her, I decided to back out of the process once and for all. She clearly had this covered.

When Melissa was offered the opportunity to row for UC Berkeley, my husband and I were thrilled to have her close by. Although the size and scope of this world-class research university was quite a shift for her, she was able to keep up with her studies and her athletics with help from tutors. Now in her late 20s, Melissa has surprised us all yet again—she has turned her attention to the family business, learning real estate (hands-on, of course) at her father's elbow. Like me, she isn't cut out for a desk job, and this business context utilizes her natural gifts and her innate craving for excitement.

Her pathway has been different from the one that I would have drawn when I held her as a baby. Looking back, I wouldn't have it any other way, and I am grateful I never used the tactic of denying her permission to participate in her favorite sports as a means of punishing her for not doing better in her academics—that would have been a disaster.

My daughter now has true ownership of her life and career. She has struggled, triumphed, and never taken her success for granted. She understands herself deeply and is able to explain herself to others. She is tough and talented. Above all, she is able to empathize with the people she meets. She knows that even though things may appear perfect on the surface, many people are struggling in ways that aren't obvious to the casual observer. She has lived this experience and knows it to be true.

Reflection

Take a little time to think honestly about your own pathway in school, in work, or in life. Was there a time when you chose a different pathway to a goal than others expected of you?

What about the paths that your child has sought over the years? Do they follow what you might consider a conventional way to proceed, to problem solve, or pursue a goal? If they used a unique approach, did it get them to the goal more quickly or was it circuitous? Unexpected? Why do you think this approach was chosen, and did it lead to the desired goal?

_____

_____

_____

_____

_____

_____

_____

_____

_____

_____

_____

_____

_____

_____

Part IV
The Way Ahead

CHAPTER 9

Success Stories

Learning that your child has some kind of learning difference can be daunting. But there are so many examples of people who have overcome these challenges—and even used them to their own advantage—that there is no real reason to feel dispirited. It might take some time to come to grips with your default mindset and to face the fact that your original parenting goals are not realistic.

I would like to share some inspiring, and often surprising, examples of enormously successful people with a range of learning differences who have thrived in business: a best-selling novelist with dyslexia; a leading economist who has trouble remembering her own PIN number; artists, actors, business leaders, and politicians who have used the risk-taking element of ADHD to propel themselves to the top; and people with dyslexia who have learned to focus on their specific strengths precisely because they were forced to confront their own weaknesses. Often, the difference of their vision or approach to life has set them apart and contributed to their success, rather than held them back. Technology, entrepreneurialism, acting, professional sports, performance arts (e.g., dancing and singing for entertainment), and fine arts (e.g., painting and sculpture) are all professional areas with large numbers of different thinkers.

The stories show what can be achieved, especially as many of the people listed here did not even have a name for their conditions at the time when they were struggling to overcome their challenges.

David Neeleman, Founder of JetBlue Airways

Neeleman didn't realize he had ADHD until he self-diagnosed in his mid-30s after his mother sent him the book *Driven to Distraction* by Edward Hallowell and John Ratey (Sellers, 2008). Neeleman's little brother had just been diagnosed with ADD (now classified as ADHD), and his mother recognized that her grown-up son also exhibited many of the same characteristics. Neeleman said, "When I got through reading, it was this huge epiphany for me. I thought, wow, that's it" (para. 2).

Neeleman continued (Sellers, 2008):

> I struggled a lot in school. I really had a hard time with standardized tests, staying focused and absorbing information from a written page into my brain. It was tough. I thought I was stupid, that I didn't have what the other kids had. In third grade, sitting inside at recess, not being able to go out, because I couldn't get my work done. That was difficult. (para. 3)

Neeleman's parents always maintained a positive attitude and emphasized to him that he had other talents that didn't necessarily need to be learned from reading (Sellers, 2008). Neeleman said that "if someone told me you could be normal or you could continue to have your ADHD, I would take ADHD" (Gilman, 2018, para. 5). The airline executive does not take medication for his condition either.

Author's note: I have read *Driven to Distraction* (Hallowell & Ratey, 2011) many times myself and given countless copies away to people who have questioned whether or not they have ADHD. For most adults, it is heartening to read about certain traits and realize that the condition is largely about brain chemistry and may have been inherited. Despite the fact that the problems still have to be dealt with, they are clearly not of a person's own making.

Richard Rogers, Architect

The English-Italian architect is the man behind the Pompidou Center in Paris, one of the most iconic buildings in the world, as well as London's Millennium Dome and the European Court of Human Rights building in Strasbourg, France.

"In my youth, in the 1940s, I was called stupid," Rogers told the Yale Center for Dyslexia and Creativity (YCDC, 2017c, para. 5). He was unable to either read or memorize his schoolwork and was always at the bottom of his class. He said, "I became very depressed. When I was young, seven or eight, I remember standing on the windowsill and saying, 'Should I jump or shouldn't I jump?'" (para. 5).

Rogers was born in Italy but was sent back to England to attend a private school outside London. He also attended a special school for a year, which he said, "saved my life because they understood my difficulties and I realized that there were other students who also had great difficulties" (YCDC, 2017c, para. 6). This encouragement was enough to give him the leg-up he needed to succeed, and he eventually attended Yale.

Rogers was close to his parents—his father was a doctor and his mother an artist. He said, "I believe it [is] important to have someone who believes in you and is supportive which in turn builds your confidence whether it is your parent, teacher or a friend" (YCDC, 2017c, para. 11). He has acknowledged his shortcomings and strengths; he does not draw as well as most architects and cannot do rote learning, but he has good spatial knowledge. Whether that is a result of his dyslexia or not is unclear.

Rogers persevered, however. It was not until his own child was diagnosed with dyslexia that he realized that he, too, had been a lifelong sufferer (YCDC, 2017c). Rogers now has an understanding of his own jagged profile, a must in selling his special set of skills. He also had two very involved and caring parents who believed in him throughout his school difficulties. Last but not least, he was able to connect with other students with similar difficulties, in the context of a specialized school.

Gavin Newsom, Governor of California

Despite being diagnosed at age 5 with dyslexia, Newsom became San Francisco's youngest elected mayor in a century in 2003, providing universal health care for poor and uninsured city residents (YCDCa, 2017a). In 2013, he published the book *Citizenville*, detailing how ordinary people could use technology to reshape and democratize governance. In 2018, he became governor of California, which has the fifth largest economy in the world.

Newsom's mother didn't tell her son that he had been diagnosed as dyslexic; she worried he might use the disability label as a crutch (YCDC, 2017a). But his kid sister did not have the same condition and breezed through school. This was hard for him as the older brother; he didn't understand why she finished her homework more quickly than he did or why his parents treated her differently about academics. Reading aloud in class was also humiliating for Newsom as a young kid. He would sit in his class,

> with my heart just sinking and pounding, hoping that that period would end and we'd get the hell out of there, and then getting up and starting to read and having everybody in the class laugh. That's when I basically gave up on any reading. I did book reports by literally reading the back of the book and just copying the text, thinking the teacher would never find out. (para. 4)

In fifth grade, he discovered in his mother's office a bunch of papers detailing his condition and his academic struggles: "That really hit home, and it explained why everyone else was running into their parents' arms after school and I was stuck in that shack behind the school every Monday, Wednesday, and Friday with four or five other students" (YCDC, 2017a, para. 2).

Knowledge of his condition didn't automatically improve Newsome's life at school (YCDC, 2017a). In high school, "the grades were bad, my self-esteem started to collapse, and I remember faking being sick all the time to avoid math class, which I just couldn't handle" (para. 5). Newsom was determined to get into college, however, and took extra summer classes to catch up. His natural ability at baseball also helped him, even after he did poorly on the SAT.

After graduating from Santa Clara University in California, Newsom worked briefly in sales and real estate before forming a company that started out as a single winery but quickly grew to include restaurants, inns, and retail clothing shops. Newsom chalked his success up to "a passion, which I decided was the secret of all success—finding that thing that motivated me beyond anything else and, with that, a willingness to fail and try new things" (YCDC, 2017a, para. 7). He has told young people:

> One of the things you learn with dyslexia is that you're going to fail often and you've got to appreciate that; as they say, failures are a portal of discovery. The secret of success is, as another dyslexic, Winston Churchill, said, "moving from failure to failure with enthusiasm." (para. 9)

According to Newsom, the key to success is discipline, which helps students solve problems and improve their self-esteem.

Author's note: Newsom is a wonderful role model for kids, especially for residents of the Bay Area. Handsome, charming, and successful, he is especially good at relating to school kids of all grades and ages. At the request of students, first at the Charles Armstrong School and later at PEN, I heard him speak to large audiences about his initial shame and now total comfort with talking about his various ways of coping with dyslexia. His main point in both presentations was that failing is a way to success for people who struggle in school. Failing, as he described it, is each person's way of learning what they are good at and enjoy.

John Irving, Novelist

Irving is one of the best-known writers in the world, who shot to fame with his fourth novel, *The World According to Garp*, which won the National Book Award in 1980. His books have sold in the millions and include *The Cider House Rules*, whose adapted screenplay won Irving an Oscar. Yet Irving has dyslexia, a fact he didn't discover until his younger son Brendan was himself diagnosed as mildly dyslexic (YCDC, 2017b).

As a student in the late 1950s and early 1960s, Irving was called "stupid" or "lazy" by his teachers at his school, yet he learned to redouble his efforts. Irving said:

> To do anything really well, you have to overextend yourself. In my case, I learned that I just had to pay twice as

much attention. I came to appreciate that in doing something over and over again, something that was never natural becomes almost second nature. You learn that you have the capacity for that, and that it doesn't come overnight. (YCDC, 2017b, para. 2)

Irving also shared his feelings about not being diagnosed and lacking the vocabulary to explain his difficulties in school (Shaywitz, 2003):

I failed a spelling test and was put in a remedial spelling class. . . . I wish I'd known, when I was a student at Exeter, that there was a word for what made being a student so hard for me; I wish I could have said to my friends that I was dyslexic. Instead I kept quiet, or—to my closest friends—I made bad jokes about how stupid I was. (p. 346)

Irving's passion for wrestling, and the encouragement of the school coach, got him through school (YCDC, 2017b). But his struggle with reading and writing ultimately gave him the tools he needed to write his long, intricate, and character-driven novels: "I have confidence in my stamina to go over something again and again no matter how difficult it is—whether it is for the fourth or fifth or eighth time" (para. 10).

Author's note: Maybe you, like me, have read some of Irving's novels. The one I am reading now is more than 800 pages long, and the sentences, characters, and themes are complex. Now that I know the extent to which he struggled in school, I am even more in awe of his ability to persevere with his writing to reach such perfection in phrasing. It is clear that he knows his own capacity for detailed thinking and writing. Not only is he willing to work around his language weakness, but he has also built a writing career on his prodigious strengths in describing scenes, feelings, and characters. Knowing his jagged profile has given him the drive to continue to produce wonderful novels.

Charles Schwab, Founder and Chairman of Charles Schwab & Co.

Like many other successful people with a learning difference, Schwab only discovered his own dyslexia when his child was diagnosed (Gilman, 2018). Schwab, the founder of America's fourth-largest brokerage firm, had struggled with reading and writing at school, although his aptitude for math and science had given him an edge. "I eventually overcame dyslexia because I was a reasonably competent kid and had a pretty outgoing personality," he said. "I could communicate with my teachers, and I asked lots of questions in class. I think that's why I became favored among teachers."

He continued, "I was always aware of the fact that I excelled with numbers, even though I struggled with reading. . . . I focused on my strengths and used my natural affinity for numbers and economics as the focus of my career" (Gilman, 2018).

Rather than hampering him, his struggles at school taught him both humility and motivation. Schwab said,

> I found something I was good at and became passionate about it. I also discovered that many skills and talents, in addition to reading ability, are as important in the making of a top executive. Character, ethics, communication skills, consistency, analytical and relationship skills. Those are important for leaders. I have some of those skills, and I work with a lot of great people who bring other strengths and talents to the table. (Gilman, 2018)

When Schwab's son was diagnosed with dyslexia, he and his wife founded The Schwab Foundation to help parents of children with learning differences find answers about how to best help their kids and to advocate on behalf of children who may need to approach education in their own way.

His advice to young people facing the same challenges that he overcame is "Find out what you can do well, focus on it, and work doubly hard" (Gilman, 2018). He said, "We all aspire to do the best we can with what we're dealt. Focus on your strengths. Don't be afraid to ask for help and to admit you need it."

Author's note: I have heard Schwab speak on this topic, and I, like most other parents of kids who struggle with learning and attention issues, am extremely grateful to him for talking openly about what worked for him in school and in life. He and his wife Helen have done so much to bring awareness and education to the subject of learning differences. Success stories like his are powerful in showing kids that they can succeed once they establish their coping skills and work-arounds.

Whoopi Goldberg, Actress

Goldberg is one of only a handful of people to have won an Emmy, a Grammy, an Oscar, and a Tony Award (i.e., an EGOT). She was also the first woman to be honored with the prestigious Mark Twain Prize for American Humor and is the author of three books, two of them for kids. Yet, like so many others in this chapter, she was once labelled "stupid" at school because of her undiagnosed dyslexia (YCDC, 2017e).

She did have an obvious talent outside of class, however: her ability to act (YCDC, 2017e). She dreamed of making her living from acting—a dream that was encouraged by her mother. "I knew I wasn't stupid, and I knew I wasn't dumb. My mother told me that," Goldberg said (para. 3).

Talent-spotted by fellow-dyslexic Stephen Spielberg while performing comedy, Goldberg received her big break in *The Color Purple* and went on to enjoy a storied career as an actress, comedienne, and writer. She said, "the challenge will always be how we see ourselves, not as folks with a handicap, but folks with an interesting perspective on everything" (The Gow School, n.d.).

Author's note: Goldberg's story is a great example of the power of a child having at least one charismatic adult in their life who will remind them of their strengths enough to keep them from identifying as deficient or unable.

Diane Swonk, Economist

By the standard metric of schools, Swonk should not be one of the nation's leading economic forecasters. "I flip numbers constantly," the former chief economist at Bank One in Chicago said (Gilman, 2018). "I joke about it in front of audiences, asking them, 'What's the difference between 1.9% and 9.1% GDP growth?' A world, actually."

Swonk, who became the youngest-ever president for the National Association for Business Economics—a post once held by Fed chairman Alan Greenspan—has dyslexia (Gilman, 2018). She often struggles to remember phone numbers or her PIN number at the ATM. But she says her mind processes information "multidimensionally rather than in linear form," giving her a rare ability to view "the endgame before others do." This has proven a distinct advantage in the fast-moving world of business and markets. That special way of seeing things "serves me extremely well for a science like economics, where, if one thing happens, another thing happens, in response," she said.

"You realize that the worst forecasting in the world takes a trajectory, a trend, and says that it will go on forever," said Swonk. She went on:

> Sometimes the recent past is just a stage, not the trajectory of where we are heading. My learning difference allows me to say, "Hey, when X happens, it doesn't mean that the next steps are going to be Y and Z." The next step may be to go back to A. (Gilman, 2018)

Her parents always taught the young Swonk to never give up and to embrace her different way of looking at the world, even if that could seem isolating at times to a youngster. "If you had to butter your bread with a chainsaw, you did," said Swonk. "You always had to find an alternative way to get things done" (Gilman, 2018).

Author's note: Swonk's story illustrates the pathways principle: When one road doesn't lead to success, look for another. There is always more than one way to reach a goal.

Daniel Radcliffe, Actor

As a child, the *Harry Potter* star was a sufferer of dyspraxia, a condition which makes it hard to plan and coordinate physical movement (Irvine, 2008). Dyspraxia can make kids appear clumsy or "out of sync" with their surroundings. They may also have trouble tying their shoelaces or mastering handwriting. When Radcliffe was 9 and was having a hard time at school, his mother encouraged him to audition for a play; she thought acting would boost his confidence. The rest, as they say, is history.

Author's note: This is one of many stories of actors for whom school didn't work well. Recently, Jennifer Lawrence told her story on *60 Minutes*. Although her path to acting differed from Radcliffe's, the feeling of being a misfit with school was a common theme.

CHAPTER 10

Case Studies

In the 20 years that I have been an activist working for a greater understanding of the nuances and needs of kids who learn differently, I have met hundreds of children, parents, educators, therapists, and psychologists, all trying to figure out what works best in dealing with learning differences.

Although each case is as different as the child or family involved, there are some common threads in successful parenting strategies: a growth mindset, individualized guidance, and a strength-based focus. Quite often, parents who use these strategies do not even realize they are doing so—they just find out what works and stick with it.

With that in mind, I want to present several case studies of families I met through my work at PEN. Each child overcame a variety of learning challenges and is now thriving in their chosen pathways. I have selected these parents and kids because there were such clear obstacles in each case for successful school experiences, yet in every story the parents found a way to bolster their children and help them to understand and own their jagged profiles.

Like the success stories of the famous people in the previous chapter, each of these stories illustrates the main principles outlined in this book.

There are many more examples emerging every day of parents helping their kids who struggle in school to thrive in life.

Case Study #1: Dennis

When I first met Dennis, he was just 3 years old. Red-headed and freckled, he was a cute little boy with a mischievous twinkle in his eye and a ready smile. His mother, Marlene, was an early volunteer for PEN and eventually went on to become its executive director. I watched Dennis grow up, as he would often come with his mom to PEN meetings, sitting in another room and playing with his toys, doing his homework, or watching a video. He would sometimes get impatient with the long hours, but he never really acted out. I found it amazing that Marlene could bring along her son so often and have him behave so well.

Dennis was well behaved and happy until he started school. In kindergarten and first grade, he attended the same private school as his sister, located in San Francisco, even though the family lived about a 40-minute drive away. Dennis was at first compliant and happy going to school with his sister, playing during recess with the other boys. He was a friendly kid, very athletic and obedient, although more introverted than a lot of the other children in his class. He didn't like it when the other boys rough-housed with him, and he started getting more and more anxious on the playground. In school, he was slow in learning to read, although he continued to try hard.

Marlene and her husband John were starting to get concerned about the tantrums Dennis would throw in the car or at home after a frustrating day in class, or during the long rides to and from school. Soon Dennis stopped going to school willingly; he started feigning sickness in the mornings so he could skip class. His anxiety grew worse at the end of second grade. He became withdrawn, sensitive, and difficult at home, which was a major shift from his usual good behavior. Marlene, who had struggled herself in school with dyslexia and some symptoms of ADHD, was quick to seek help for Dennis, just in case he had inherited some of her school difficulties. She had him evaluated by an educational therapist who told her there was nothing wrong with Dennis.

As he moved into the third grade, Dennis became even more frustrated with the long drive and the lack of physical space that the city school provided. He talked to his mom about transferring to the school in his hometown, which had a larger faculty and where some of the boys from his hometown baseball team went.

Because of Dennis's slowness to learn how to read, his mom had him evaluated again by a psychologist who diagnosed him with sensory processing disorder and inattentive type ADHD, both of which caused symptoms that inhibited his ability to learn. Counselling was prescribed for his ADHD symptoms, which mostly manifested in a need for control and a lack of flexibility, both of which were exacerbated by the stark contrast with his mom's extremely flexible attitude toward life. The psychologist gave Marlene and Dennis an analogy of how they operated on a daily basis that helped them understand each other: Dennis was like a train, going steadily along the track on rails that are fixed in space and don't provide for quick changes in direction; Marlene was like a Volkswagen Beetle, able to zip in and out of traffic and change direction frequently.

For the sensory integration issues, sessions with an occupational therapist (OT) were prescribed. Both Marlene and Dennis felt that the evaluation and the following interventions had a positive effect on their relationship. Dennis felt much better with some of the actions shown to the family by the OT—she showed Marlene how to brush Dennis's skin and cover him with a heavy blanket, among some other strategies for calming him down when he got frustrated. The sessions and the brushing were very helpful to his moods and calming him down. He learned how to take better control of his outbursts by asking his mom for some of the techniques they had learned and also through talk therapy, which provided him with the words and strategies to deal with his anger. One such strategy was having Dennis draw pictures of himself in various stages of being out of control; rather than scream and jump around, he learned to hold these signs up to his family members when he felt a tantrum coming on. He and his mom both laugh about these signs now, which are still in his garage (in case he ever needs them again)!

Dennis is a young adult now and I recently talked with him about his memories of the difficulties he had in school, how he felt about his struggles then and now, and what, or who, actually helped him the most. I was surprised at how comfortable he was talking about his earlier struggles. He was very clear about what—and who—helped him during those times: his mom and dad, but mostly his mom because he was with her more then. She listened to him from an early age, gave him the freedom to make choices, and made him feel like he had some measure of control.

This freedom was shown by Dennis's attendance at many different schools over the years. When he wanted to change elementary schools and made a reasonable argument for doing so, his parents helped him make the change. Only one time did this turn out to be a decision he regretted; he went back to his old school only to transfer the next year to yet another one. He said he learned from that mistake and did better with his requests for change as a result.

His first choice for his freshman year of high school was an all-boys parochial school with a resource program to help him with his strategies for focus, as well as a wonderful athletic program in which he was a star in several sports. He did very well in his freshman year, but as his interest in sports waned and he became more interested in cooking and guitar, he again asked to transfer schools, this time to an experimental program in a city just south of San Francisco. There, the students have much more control over their own education and can pick electives and engage in self-study courses. Dennis thrived in this school, as it appealed to his sense of having more control over his education and offered him the freedom to pursue his interests as they evolved.

As a result, Dennis was accepted to early admission at Hampshire College, a small liberal arts college in Amherst, MA. When I asked why he chose that school, he told me that it doesn't give grades (he finds grades unhelpful to developing his learning abilities), classes are small, and curriculum choice is entirely up to the student. Dennis has gone from an athlete, to an aspiring chef, to a scholar over the last 4 years, and is now a young man who is very comfortable in his own skin, and whose parents beam with pride at what he has become. They still have a close relationship.

Case Study #2: Gary

Lucille and Andrew's 12 years of guiding their son Gary through the learning difference journey is a wonderful example of how a child can be transformed. Gary went from self-selected outlier in the early school years to academic success story by the time he was in high school, where he became engaged with his school and came out of his shell to develop a group of friends with whom he is very comfortable. His parents worked with him every step of the way from the first indications that he was not a good fit with his school, striving to understand what he needed in an academic environment.

When Lucille and Andrew visited Gary's preschool to watch the kids graduate from one level to the next, they were surprised to see that 4-year-old Gary was not part of the lineup of happy kids, but rather stayed far away from the group—a loner, not interacting with the other kids or engaging in the fun activities. This was the first sign to Lucille, a psychologist, that Gary was different from his peers. She began to watch more closely for other signs of upcoming school difficulties.

While Gary was in preschool, his lack of a hand dominance—he was neither left- nor right-handed—was discovered by an occupational therapist who did monthly visitations to the school to screen each child for potential difficulties. She also reported that he was reluctant to cross his midline when writing or drawing (i.e., he would switch hands halfway through drawing or writing a line on paper)—a fairly serious observation when a child is developing fine motor skills. The therapist worked with Gary for the rest of the year to bring his motor skills more in line with expectations for his age group.

When he went to a public school for kindergarten, Gary continued in his loner style, more comfortable with his own play ideas than joining in with the other kids' games. When the other kids were learning numbers and letters, and eventually learning to read, Gary was slipping further behind. By the time he was in second grade, he had become an anxious and frustrated little boy. He insisted that writing hurt his hand, and he was aware that he was not reading and developing the skills that other kids in his grade were capable of.

When Lucille asked the school to provide an evaluation for learning differences, she was told to wait until Gary was further along in school. The school staff was sure he would pick up his skills on his own. But Gary's anxiety was a concern, and the longer he was allowed to fail, the worse his anxiety and declining self-esteem became. On her own, Lucille sought reading support from her local reading clinic, where a very skilled tutor spent a year teaching him to read. This tutor informally diagnosed Gary with dyslexia and suggested a full psych-ed evaluation.

Even though Gary was reading a little, he began to show his anger and frustration at home by sticking even more to himself and insisting on wearing all black, which made him stand out even more from his peers at an early age. (His mother insisted that 8-year-old goths were a rarity in their small town.)

When Gary was in second grade, his parents decided to pay for a private psych-ed evaluation themselves because the public school did not want to provide it. They showed the report to the learning specialists and the principal of the public school, and asked for an Individualized Education Program (IEP) for Gary based on the test results.

When the school still refused the request for an IEP, Lucille argued with the school's interpretation of the psych-ed results—namely that Gary was fine and did not need any academic intervention. A friend of Lucille, who happened to be another PEN board member, suggested that she and I go to the next meeting that Lucille had with the school principal. Luckily, the principal was familiar with PEN and welcomed us to join their meeting. We were going there as a group to talk about the options Gary had to get the services he qualified for.

The principal was up front with us and stated that he didn't have the manpower to provide special services for Gary. He stated to me that his job as principal of a public school was to see that all of the kids passed with at least a C. Given Gary's high scores in cognitive tests, his parents expected him to be more developed in line with his abilities. Because of his documented learning differences—dyslexia, dyscalculia, and ADHD—it was clear that he could not achieve the grades he deserved without support from the school. The principal suggested to Lucille that if she wanted Gary to be educated to his capacity, she should enroll him in a private school where he could get more attention.

At this point, Lucille realized that it was up to her and her husband to provide the education that they required for their son. We left knowing that we had not convinced the principal to give Gary an IEP for the services he needed to succeed in his classes. Instead of fighting further, Lucille and Andrew chose to enroll Gary in a school where he would get the attention he needed in areas where his learning differences were holding him back.

At the new school, which focused on kids with learning differences, Gary began to read more confidently. Although math had never been his favorite subject, he passed the subject while there and began to see himself as a learner. Although no one would have predicted it, Gary started to develop a real interest and strength in writing. Essays and creative pieces were his specialties, and his confidence in these skills began to grow during middle school. He use a word-processing program for spelling and basic grammar, so he was no longer held back in his ability to express himself on paper. He attended this school from grades 4–8 and was admitted to a private boys' high school, where he became a strong student with a 3.5

GPA with the help of the resource center. He learned to ask for help from the tutors there. Recently, he started studying at the college of his choice, a small liberal arts college in Oregon. He is still undecided about his major but insists that whatever his future holds, writing will be a part of it.

He credited the tutoring he received from a college student, who worked with him on his homework from the seventh grade through high school, as one of the best interventions he had. As often happens, the young man was not only able to help Gary during school, but also developed a long-term friendship with him; they share many interests and are still in regular communication. The tutor is also dyslexic, so he became a wonderful role model for Gary. Lucille insisted that the young tutor also saved her relationship with her son, giving him someone other than his parents to share his interests and daily frustrations with.

Case Study #3: Courtney

Courtney was Mary and Scott's firstborn, and she passed all of the milestones as explained by the books on child development: She walked at 11 months, developed speech between years 1–2, and asked to learn to ski at 2-and-a-half years old at a toddlers' ski school, where the children play inside for half of the class and are taught to ski down a very short slide with a green felt carpet on it during the other half. After a few days of this, Courtney complained to her parents that she hated art and "skiing" on a carpet, and insisted on learning to ski on snow. So her dad taught her how to ski when she was still very little. She loved it and seemed fearless.

That same year, Courtney started preschool for 2 hours a day, 2 days per week. She seemed to like it, went enthusiastically on the designated days, and made a couple of friends there. Her parents had two conferences during the year, and Mary was surprised by the feedback she received during the first 15-minute talk: Courtney, according to the teacher, was very young-acting, was not cooperative during circle time, spilled her water on purpose, and needed a lot of attention from the teacher. Mary disregarded this information, as her friends with older kids joked that as soon as their children went to school, the negative feedback started.

The next year, Courtney attended a much more structured and serious preschool that a lot of Mary's friends had recommended. With just 4 hours per week involved, Mary didn't think it was enough time to have much impact on her daughter; she just trusted that this was a popular preschool.

When Mary and Scott visited their daughter in her classroom late in the school year, they were ushered into a tiny closet-sized room with a two-way mirror, where they watched in quiet disbelief as their little one failed to participate in the activities with the other kids. At the end of this 30-minute display, the head of the preschool told Mary and Scott that she wanted them to "see firsthand what we have been seeing in your daughter all year" and that Courtney would have to repeat that same class the next year. They were dismayed and speechless at this offhand judgment but decided that the preschool head was an educator and therefore must know what she was doing.

The following year, their daughter repeated the same grade and became even less responsive in her class. In October, at the school's suggestion, Mary and Scott hired a child psychiatrist to observe Courtney in the class and give a recommendation. This led to a diagnosis that their 4-year-old was "clinically depressed" and a recommendation that Courtney be put back into her original class with kids of her own age, in addition to 6 months of play therapy. This feedback was confusing to both Courtney and her mother. Mary had lost confidence in the opinion of the school's headmaster by that point. Another parent, who was herself a teacher, told Mary, "I just don't think Ms. D. likes or 'gets' your daughter." At her suggestion, Mary decided to transfer preschools.

The next year Mary and Scott moved Courtney to a school that had an extra class for those not quite ready to move to kindergarten. This was a recommendation from their pediatrician, whose advice they had sought. The new preschool had a more play-based program, and Courtney settled in quickly, making friends with several of the other students. From there, Courtney was accepted into two academic all-girls elementary schools. Of the two, Mary and Scott chose the one that had the reputation of being more "developmental." The other program had a reputation for pushing girls too fast through the early years; several friends had daughters who were already seeing tutors. Mary and Scott wanted a more relaxed yet academic program.

Courtney's first teacher was experienced and savvy about the variety of readiness levels exhibited by the different girls in the kindergarten class. She took Mary aside almost immediately at the start of school and told her, "Your daughter certainly listens to her own drummer, and she is a wonderful addition to this class," which Mary took as a compliment. The teacher later told Mary and Scott that Courtney's motor skills were a bit behind the other girls' and suggested some exercises and an extra PE class to help her catch up.

When Courtney was in the second grade, her parents decided to have her tested for learning differences at the suggestion of her teachers, several of whom assured them she was a bright and perceptive little girl but still a little slow in learning to read and keeping up with the lessons in the classroom. Courtney was a "little distractible" or "dreamy," often staring out the window during class time.

The evaluation would have been very confusing to the couple had they not been referred to an experienced psychiatrist and education consultant who had worked with all of the cities' schools and with her own five children. This psychiatrist was a game changer. Without showing Mary and Scott the report, she spent 15 minutes telling them her interpretation of it: "Your daughter has a learning profile that is not the best fit for the school you have selected; however, if you send her to a different school, she is likely to fall through the cracks as an average student, despite the fact that she is of superior intelligence. Because of the inconsistency in her different skill sets, she will take several years to fill the gaps in the areas where she is currently, at age 8, behind her peers." She went on to say, "It will be up to you to fill the gaps for her by providing support, like scaffolding, until she is caught up enough to do it for herself."

Mary and Scott provided various interventions for Courtney in her early school years, like letting her dictate papers as Mary typed, offering her extra time for processing on tests, and letting her give answers on a test orally instead of writing them down. Courtney began to thrive in the middle school years and went on to a small, individualized program for high school where she continued to excel academically while finding her interests and talents as an honor student and swimmer. When Courtney went to a medium-sized Division I school as a walk-on track team member, she was on her way to feeling in control of her life. She graduated with a B.A. in sociology and continued for the next 6 years to obtain her Ph.D. in the same field. She has been in practice for the last 5 years, working with disenfranchised families and their children with autism. She said she has found her calling.

When Mary looked back on those years, when she was so confused by what she was and wasn't hearing from the schools, she realized that she was afraid to ask questions—at first at the preschool and then in the early years of elementary school—because she trusted that the teachers knew all there was to know about the kids they were teaching. This, as she found, was a naïve viewpoint. Without the evaluation and help of the psychiatrist, Mary is not sure what Courtney's outcome would have been.

Case Study #4: Brad

As a 5-year-old, Brad was a joyful, inquisitive, and confident little guy. For Halloween he told his mother, Mary Ann, that he wanted to be a king and held his head high as he walked around the block in his homemade costume with a red velvet cape, cardboard crown, and scepter. His costume suited his confidence.

All of that confidence ebbed quickly when Brad moved from preschool into kindergarten and grade school. He started having trouble with letters and words. From first to third grade, the demands of writing and reading continued to increase for Brad. His frustration showed in the classroom when he chewed through erasers and pencils out of sheer anxiety. He would often hold in his emotions until he got home, where he routinely came unglued, yelling or crying.

Finally, his teachers suggested that Brad be tested for learning differences in the third grade. When Brad talked to staff members at school, he told them that he was "stupid." This broke his mother's heart because she knew how bright he was, which was confirmed by the testing. But somehow, all Brad knew about himself was that reading and writing were much harder for him than his peers.

When the evaluation showed that Brad had dyslexia, Mary Ann's reaction was to ask for more information about this condition and what she could do to help him. She scoured the Internet for information, spending hours searching for information to understand and help her son, but was unable to distinguish the truth from incorrect or misleading information. She wasn't sure if she could trust her own research.

She tried reaching out to other parents whose kids might have the same issue, but to her surprise, most of them were unwilling to talk about their children's struggles. She realized there was a huge stigma associated with learning differences. Like a lot of other parents, Mary Ann found herself alone in her search for ways to help Brad. Meanwhile, her son's self-esteem continued to slide as his frustration grew. In desperation, Mary Ann spent hours tracking down experts and eventually struck gold when she found a reading expert who explained to her in plain language why her son was struggling and what kind of help he needed.

When Brad's IEP meeting was scheduled, both parents went. This proved to be the turning point for Brad's mom and dad to get on the same page about how to help Brad at home so that school would go better for him. The purpose of the meeting was to see if the results of the evaluation qualified him for special education services. There were 10 adults gathered around the table in the school conference room. Mary Ann was hugely relieved when they all talked about Brad's school difficulties and suggested that they, as a team, wanted to help him to learn. They outlined a plan for the kind of support they needed to provide for Brad and became partners in providing it.

By the time Brad was about to move to middle school, he had become more comfortable in the classroom with his accommodations and had begun to excel in math. Mary Ann asked Brad what he thought about moving to middle school, which was located in a separate building from the lower grades. When they went together to see the space where he would go for his special education classes, they talked about how these classes were held in the basement, which meant being separated from his class for hours at a time. He was also concerned that his isolation in the basement would cause him to miss some of the elective classes he was looking forward to taking.

In her constant quest to make things easier for Brad, Mary Ann found a school that specialized in teaching kids with dyslexia. This was another turning point; Brad was finally surrounded by kids who shared his struggles and was much more comfortable in a learning environment where he didn't stand out.

When the new school suggested testing Brad more comprehensively with a full psych-ed evaluation, Mary Ann was deeply worried that he might have yet another learning difference to cope with. To her surprise, though, Brad didn't object to the extra testing; in fact, he was afraid that maybe his dyslexia had "gone away." He had become very comfortable with his talents and with his label. When the new evaluation showed that he also had ADHD, his mom sobbed secretly in her car as she realized that Brad now had another challenge to face. Before telling Brad the outcome of the testing, she went on the search for more information, just as she done with the earlier diagnosis of dyslexia. She learned that these two conditions often accompany each other.

When she finally shared the news with Brad, he was once again relieved to hear that there was a biological reason for his continued struggles with attention and organization. He was confident he could overcome them as he had with dyslexia. He didn't see the diagnosis as yet another challenge to face, as he had already realized he was struggling with these issues. Now they finally had a name: ADHD.

There was another IEP meeting, which Mary Ann and her husband attended with Brad. They realized they could help Brad with strategies and modifications given for ADHD and dyslexia at home, organizing his assignments and talking through where to start on his homework—something that was always a struggle for him. Together, the family looked at other kinds of interventions, like medication, and ultimately decided against them. The strategies they were using at home were sufficient scaffolding for Brad to succeed.

When Brad began to thrive, first in middle school and then at high school, with his accommodations, Mary Ann reflected on how hard it had been for her to find reliable and helpful information to help her son, and also how helpful it was to have a partner in the journey through the maze of learning differences.

Recently I talked to Mary Ann and Brad to follow up on what he is doing now. Brad is a junior in college and an avid speed skater with a coaching certification. He recently called his mom to tell her about a third-grade boy he is coaching. The boy's parents heard that Brad had learning and attention issues in school and reached out to him to ask for advice about how to help their son, who has similar issues and is struggling in school. Brad listened intently to what they were telling him about the boy's sliding self-esteem as a result of kids making fun of his efforts to read aloud. Brad is all too aware of how reading and language problems can make a kid stand out in a regular classroom.

As he talked to the parents, Brad realized that they knew very little about dyslexia and thought it might just be a vision issue. When they learned that it is a neurobiological condition that needs more support and understanding than just glasses, Brad took advantage of the teaching moment and encouraged them to connect with other parents for support and to visit Understood's website (https://www.understood.org/en).

For Brad, the experience was a turning point. Although he is comfortable with his challenges, explaining them to other people hasn't always been a positive experience, so he had largely stopped trying. For the sake of the boy he coaches, he knew he had to try to make the parents understand how to help their son. His empathy for that boy pushed him to intervene, and the feedback from the parents was positive. I am sure they are grateful for Brad's help in understanding more about what their son is going through at school. Brad is proud to have helped this one family, and Mary Ann is prouder than ever of him.

When I asked Brad about his experience growing up with learning differences, he said that going to a school where he met other kids with dyslexia turned things around for him. He felt more comfortable with kids his age who were able to talk about their challenges with reading and writing, and he was amazed when he realized "that there were so many kids like me." At that point, he was truly able to be himself in school, where he learned the basic tools of language and found out what dyslexia was. That school helped him learn how to explain his learning style to others.

He also credited his parents' support in helping him to identify and work through his school struggles, always pushing him forward when he was ready. Both Brad and his mom agreed that sports like karate and competitive speed skating gave him a physical outlet that eased anxiety and attention issues while giving him the recognition he deserved.

Now a junior in college with a major in mechanical engineering, Brad is considering a graduate school program in the same subject.

Case Study #5: Barry

Barry's mother, Anne, intuitively felt that her son had struggled since shortly after his birth. Early on, Barry showed signs of delayed gross and fine motor milestones. In addition, the quality of his physical movement was somewhat uncoordinated. He rolled as a mode of transportation prior to cross-crawling, and he was slightly hypotonic, meaning that his muscle tone at rest was more lax than normal, which included his facial muscles. Unless he was smiling or crying, it was difficult to tell what was going on in his mind. He didn't walk unassisted until about 21 months, and was grossly delayed and uncoordinated in running, jumping, etc.

Because Barry displayed some challenges at an early age, he spent first and second grade at a specialized school, where he and his classmates spent the first 2 hours of each day in movement—running, doing occupational therapeutic types of play, etc.—before sitting down at their desks. Running around the playground with his peers was challenging because he was not as fast or agile as the others. Although he did begin to read at this school, his progress was slow, but it was steady enough that he went back to his original school in third grade. His parents and teachers watched closely for signs of learning disabilities and had frequent meetings to discuss his progress.

By the end of fourth grade, Barry would have occasional meltdowns; he would be in tears, feeling discouraged and "stupid" and saying that he was not able to learn at his school. He required his parents' assistance with all of his homework, although he wished to work independently.

That summer, he underwent a full neuro-psych evaluation. His main diagnoses were dyslexia, dysgraphia, and slow processing. Although his reading speed and decoding were very weak, his comprehension and depth of understanding were very strong. His verbal abilities were way above average, but his fine motor and writing abilities were extremely poor. (He still has difficulty reading his own handwriting.) The psychologist who did the assessment affirmed to him that he was a very bright young man, that his difficulties were intense and real, and that with the right support, he could thrive nonetheless. These diagnoses were fitting and affirming of both his and his parents' experiences.

Barry's parents spent his fifth-grade year working toward positive solutions and changes, speaking with his teachers, with him, and with friends and acquaintances who were expert educational therapists. From January through June, Barry went to his school for part of each day and worked with educational therapists for the remainder of the day. This helped tremendously but was labor intensive for his mother (who drove him to school, tutoring, therapists, etc.), and it was not sustainable beyond fifth grade. It was also very expensive. His parents explored other schools, and by the end of that year, Barry had been accepted to the Charles Armstrong School, an excellent program for students with language-based learning disabilities, which would change his life.

That spring, Anne took Barry to the first EdRev (Education Revolution), the annual conference at the Giants' Stadium put on by the Parents Education Network. This event was another life changer for him. Sitting in the stands of his beloved Giants' stadium, Barry's face lit up as the he listened to dynamic movers and shakers in the learning differences world, especially Jonathan Mooney, an inspiring, charismatic man with ADHD who had an unforgettable message. Barry suddenly realized that he was not alone in his learning differences, nor stupid; he just thinks and learns differently. This world *needs* people who think differently. This day would change the course of his life.

Although switching schools was initially terrifying for Barry, the change had an enormously positive impact. CAS's focus on remediation through appropriate instruction helped bring Barry up to grade level and beyond. He came to understand his strengths and challenges, and worked on strengthening his areas of challenge through focus, hard work, and self-advocacy. He began to utilize the assistive technology that would help him to thrive academically. He was exposed to numerous exceptional and inspiring adults with learning differences. His self-esteem grew as he came to see himself as a highly capable young man who encouraged and inspired others. He graduated from eighth grade with the school's highest award for academic excellence and leadership.

Although Barry is not the stellar athlete he may wish he were, his early gross and fine motor challenges have receded far into the background. He is a thriving and strong young adult at the University of California, Davis, working diligently toward a life of empowering young people so they do not have to go through the hardships he endured. Barry is committed to helping to change the world of education for people with diverse learning profiles. He has not outgrown his learning differences but has learned how to work with them and to be academically successful through metacognition, hard work, self-advocacy, and appropriate assistive technology.

In his spare time, he founded and directs the Davis chapter of Eye to Eye (https://eyetoeyenational.org), is a young leader for the National Center for Learning Differences, advocates for different learners around the country, and is an intern for a local politician running for superintendent of instruction for California.

Author's note: Of all of the success stories I have personally witnessed, Barry's has a special place in my heart. I asked him to accompany me to a presentation at Microsoft when he had just completed his freshman year at UC Davis. We carpooled down and back to the site, more than an hour's drive from San Francisco, and stayed for about 4 hours, ending with a group lunch. I couldn't believe the young man that Barry had become. Tall and handsome, dressed in an Oxford shirt and khakis, he was self-assured and comfortable in his own skin. He charmed all of us at lunch. He often expresses his gratitude to his parents, especially his mom, for all of the extra support she provided him in his early years. He also considers finding a community of other kids who learn differently one of his biggest game changers.

CHAPTER 11

The Coming
Revolution

It is one thing to discuss learning differences in the relative safety of schools and colleges. It is quite another to talk openly about them in the workplace. I was amazed to hear so many people publicly sharing their experiences at the second annual Neurodiversity Conference, held in 2013 at the Microsoft Technology Center in Mountain View, CA.

I went with my friend and fellow PEN board member, Stu Schader, who is also a founder of the conference. Stu is dyslexic and never went to college. He opted instead to launch a career in technology right out of high school. Such decisions are not uncommon in Silicon Valley, where I often meet people who followed different pathways to success, or who found school difficult, boring, or just plain irrelevant to their interests, before finding their niche in the world of tech.

Being at a conference where gainfully employed adults were outing themselves as having learning disabilities was quite an eye-opener. I was aware of the risk a lot of them were taking just by attending; most employers, even in Silicon Valley, are still not on board with the Science of Individuality's jaggedness concept. The fact that some people are just more jagged than others isn't widely accepted in the world at large. Every day, in performance reviews and considerations for promotion, people who learn differently are assessed according to conventional standards that don't—or shouldn't—apply to them.

Jaggedness in the Workplace

In every office there are employees who seem different or are challenged by tasks that come easily to their colleagues. They may seem disorganized, unable to complete some tasks in a timely manner, or lacking in obvious social skills. Yet they possess other skills and abilities that can often prove vital to the success of a team's efforts.

These individuals face many tough decisions in the workplace: Should those with dyslexia expose themselves by asking for job information on tape, or ask to use speech-to-text technology to complete reports? Should those with ASD explain their social discomforts and give their team some insights into strategies that might help?

At PEN, we advocated the following process for students and parents: Educate, Collaborate, Empower. In fact, this was the shortened form of our mission statement. Starting in the mid-2000s, some companies in Silicon Valley, like LinkedIn, Google, and Microsoft, began to form affinity groups for people who felt somewhat marginalized because of their different brains and work habits. This trend made it clear that the same process used by PEN for children at school could apply for adults in careers.

In technology companies, the edges of individual jaggedness can be extreme. According to the *Financial Times*, there are many more employees in this particular field who have ASD, ADHD, and dyslexia than in a normal population (Ahuja, 2014). Some speculate that this is because people who have high edges in science, math, and technology often have challenges that could have been called learning disabilities when they were in school. But these folks excel in their high-powered workplaces. These employees are gifted, creative thinkers and problem solvers. Perhaps they are employed by these tech companies *because* of their learning differences, not despite them. Some research favors the idea that neurological differences are usually accompanied by gifts (Eide & Eide, 2011).

Challenges as Strengths

A number of business leaders have attributed at least part of their success to their learning differences. Ned Hallowell, the ADHD guru, talks in most of his presentations about unwrapping the gifts of ADHD. When Johan Wiklund, a professor of entrepreneurship at Syracuse University's Whitman School of Management, was diagnosed with ADHD in 2012, he decided to launch a study into how ADHD may actually help business leaders (Belanger, 2017). He concluded that the intense focus that those with ADHD can muster for projects they are passionate about often cancels out the concomitant problems of inattentiveness; at the same time, the hyperactivity element of the condition allows them to commit themselves to deals and projects when other colleagues might falter.

Added to that, the impulsivity that is characteristic of many people with ADHD allows them to operate fearlessly, and with a clear head, in high-risk environments that would intimidate many neurotypical entrepreneurs who may overthink, hesitate, or simply be scared off from a business proposition. An example of a risk-taker in business is Richard Branson, the Virgin Group chief, one-time giant in the recording industry, and now space entrepreneur. He also has ADHD and dyslexia.

As for autism, there is an increasing awareness that if the right environment is created, people with autism may actually have an advantage over others, especially in a world dominated by technology where the traditional office environment is less important.

Thinking Differently

About a decade ago, Thorkil Sonne, the technical director at a Danish telecoms company, learned that his 3-year-old son had autism; however, he saw in the boy an aptitude for mathematics and memory skills that were so unusual that he knew they would serve his son well in technology. Sonne quit his job and started his own company Specialisterne—or "Specialists" in Danish—that recruited workers with autism and found them tech jobs that suited their abilities. Instead of conducting interviews, which people with autism may find intimidating, the company often asks candidates to build something—a robot or a model—from a LEGO kit, which is far more suited both to their abilities and to the jobs they perform. The company has expanded to the United States and elsewhere in recent years, finding people who may lack the social skills necessary for an office environment yet have highly developed abilities in programming and software testing. Sometimes the jobs can be painstaking and repetitive, and therefore beyond the concentration and observation powers of neurotypical people. Sonne compared people with ASD to dandelions—they can be seen as weeds on the lawn, or they can be embraced as spring greens and used in salads. "Every one of us has the power to decide," he said, "do we see a weed, or do we see an herb?" (Cook, 2012).

Several scientific studies have shown a superior ability in autistic minds to notice minute details, mentally rotate complex three-dimensional structures, and distinguish between sounds. One study (Howlin et al., 2009) concluded that around a third of males with autism have some kind of outstanding ability. People with autism also concentrate more of their brain's resources on visual processing and less on tasks like planning and impulse control, making them up to 40% faster at problem solving (Khazan, 2015).

In a rapidly changing economy where technology, robotics, and artificial intelligence are playing an increasingly important role—and where many people now have the ability to work remotely from the privacy of their own homes—there are clear niches opening up for people with ASD. Peter Thiel, the billionaire cofounder of PayPal, has even said that Asperger's syndrome, a mild form of autism, "happens to be a plus for innovation and creating great companies," allowing people to think differently in a highly competitive industry where new ideas and approaches are the keys to innovation, and where conformity or a herd mentality can doom a company to irrelevance (as cited in Baer, 2015, para. 9).

Workplace Opportunities for Different Thinkers

Tyler Cowen, an economist at George Mason University, argued that with the new economy demanding ever greater specialization of specific skills, especially those in the areas of science, engineering, and mathematics, the prospects for employment for workers with autism are only likely to improve (Cook, 2012).

Take, for example, the case of Joel Bissmire, a young man with autism who was bullied at school and then abused by colleagues at the fast food restaurant where he worked in Brisbane, Australia. One time, his colleagues locked him in a freezer and flicked him so hard with rubber bands that he bled. Yet, with the help of Specialisterne, whose reach is starting to spread around the world, Joel landed a job as a cybersecurity consultant at Hewlett-Packard, where he uses his strong analytical and mathematical skills, attention to detail, and ability to carry out repetitive tasks to secure their computer products (Bavas, 2015).

To help these newly integrated workers fit in to workplaces where they might once have been excluded, many of the big companies in the tech world (e.g., Google, Microsoft, LinkedIn) have been quietly starting affinity groups for different types of thinkers. In addition to helping these different thinkers find and support one another, the groups educate employees about some of the personality quirks that might accompany the gifts that employees with autism bring to work with them.

Benefits of Outing Learning Differences at Work

I recently met a young man at Google who introduced himself to me as an "autistic programmer." He had just appeared in an educational video that had gone viral throughout the company.

"I am now about as out as you can get, in terms of my autism," he told me, explaining that "coming out" was worth it. Being open had helped his group change the working environment for others whose social skills and quirky habits were often misunderstood or judged harshly. He explained to me that after he'd been at Google for 3 years, his boss gave him a review that emphasized his need to make eye contact with others and be more social when he was working with his team. He had to educate his boss about the traits that many people with autism display as a result of their neurological makeup. His boss apologized and realized that a better approach would be to educate the other employees, rather than ask this employee to change his personality.

The Education Revolution

When I look at the way these brave neurodiverse folks are creating an atmosphere of accommodation, discussion, and even celebration around different ways of learning and thinking in their workplaces, I can't help but compare it to the process we parents went through in founding PEN.

Along with many other parents, we believe we are part of a grassroots revolution in education—one that is already changing the way people with learning differences can approach school and, ultimately, the workplace. Already many schools are adopting our strength-based, individualized approach, even if the language used may differ from place to place. For this reason, we named our annual meetings in San Francisco *EdRev*, a contraction of "Education Revolution." Our first gathering was held in spring of 2009 in AT&T (now Oracle) Park, the home of the San Francisco Giants, and has been repeated there every year since. (Trusting our intuition that kids wouldn't want to attend a function at a school on a Saturday, we chose a ballpark because of its novelty as a conference site and its advertisement of "An Unconventional Space for Unconventional Events.") EdRev, now subtitled, "A day to think a little differently," brings together a whole community of students from across the nation who learn differently, as well as the family members and professionals who support them.

The day always features an inspirational keynote speaker, a wide range of workshops, an exhibitor fair, and a student celebration. But most important is the experience attendees have—many for the first time ever—of being part of a community that supports students who learn differently and celebrates their strengths. Every year brings new testimonials from families about the transformational effect of attending. This truly unique event now attracts visitors from across the country each year.

For example, I received the following e-mail from a first-time attendee in 2016.

Dewey,

I hope you are well. I just wanted to THANK YOU again for inviting my family to the EdRev event earlier this year. It was truly an eye-opening, life-changing experience for the whole family! Especially for my husband who, as you might remember, was in denial that our daughter even had a learning difference.

After returning home . . . we soon scouted a school for children with learning difference[s] and found one we really liked.

Our daughter has started this school year at Center Academy in Tampa and loves it! She is doing really well! And life at home has changed dramatically. The school has a no homework policy unless the child does not finish their work in class. And we love that part!

The stress and anxiety that school once generated is in the past!

She has even made new friends, she's confident and does not have to worry about being judged or being bullied in this school.

I remember sharing with you how my daughter had asked a teacher a math question and was told by her teacher that "the question could not be answered because they were not allow to teach past her grade level (even in the advanced gifted program)."

Not so in her new school! She needed to be challenged so they allowed her to learn with the fifth graders. A few weeks later she tested out of fourth-grade math. This blew my husband away!

The first report card just came out and it's the first time she has ever earned straight A's and made the Principal's list!

It might have [been] many years later before my husband would have accepted my daughter's learning difference and finally [made] the decision to change schools if it weren't for EdRev.

—Thank you!

The programs and principles we developed during 15 years of PEN have been proven to work, demonstrably improving academic and life outcomes for students with learning and attention differences, as well as for their parents. In 2013, we launched a strategic planning process, led by specialists in the field, to uncover what exactly lay behind their effectiveness and how we could make our model replicable for other groups of parents around the country. The result was what is known in the nonprofit world as a "theory of change," an underlying set of assumptions about how social change occurs. Our theory of change defines how we achieve these outcomes and the role that our work plays in shaping progress. The following is what we uncovered.

PEN'S THEORY OF CHANGE

If parents and their children who learn differently . . .

- are exposed to the latest learning research and apply that research to daily decisions;
- connect face-to-face with each other, share resources to meet common needs, and create a community working together for student success; and
- collaborate with professionals who also strive to apply the latest learning research;

then . . .

- the chances increase that children with learning and attention differences will reach their full potential and become all they can be.

I provide this theory of change here in the hope that anyone approaching these issues in their family or their community will find PEN's model worthy of emulation. To me, the principles that PEN is based on are self-evident, but they are also proven by years of success for our students and our growth as an organization. In essence, PEN is a real-time demonstration of a community putting the variability mindset into practice. This means placing the student voice at the center of the conversation, emphasizing the amazing strengths of students who learn differently, and forging collaborative relationships to support each student.

I believe that PEN, in its forward-looking approach, grounded in the ideas of universal variability and personalized education, represented the future of community work in this field. It offered a successful model for parents and community groups around the country. In 2017, PEN merged with Children's Health Council in Palo Alto, CA. There is a need for more organizations around the country that provide a community for parents of children with learning differences to get the support they need.

After so many years of dealing with a culture of secrecy and stigma around accommodations for individuals who learn differently, more schools—and enlightened managers in the workplace—are now leading the charge for change. Productivity rises with effectiveness when students, workers, and team members feel supported and understood.

The only real risk for parents is inaction. I understand your concerns; you may feel paralyzed by the task ahead, or you think it will take time to absorb these lessons and master the ways to put it all into action. Yes, you'll make mistakes along the way—everybody does. But the only real mistake is to not show up as a parent. Simply by exposing yourself to the new and effective ways of dealing with these challenges, you have already taken the first step. The next chapter provides a list of tools to conquer your doubts and give your child the chance to successfully make their way in the world, using all of their talents and thriving on your support.

Thank you for reading this book. I sincerely hope you have learned something from it that will help you help your child. All children are deserving and capable of having a happy and successful life. Please check out my website at https://www.deweyrosetti.com. Or e-mail me at deweyrosetti2020@gmail.com with questions, concerns, and additional ideas to make parenting struggling kids a successful journey.

Recommended Resources

My early parenting certainly had negative effects until I got the help I needed from more positive research findings about kids who learn differently. The authors and thinkers whose books and speaking tours helped me the most were those who had practical day-to-day experience with kids just like mine, and like the thousands of other kids I have met over the years. These people continue to see the positive, strength-based aspects of having a learning difference.

While searching for information that will help your child understand their own jaggedness, pathways, and best context, you will encounter a disproportionate amount of information that emphasizes fixing what's wrong. I cannot overstate how important it is to understand all of the research that points to the *positive* side of neurodiversity and the hopefulness of parenting a child who thinks differently than they are being taught in so many mainstream schools.

This chapter compiles a list of the researchers, educators, activists, and organizations I have found to be most helpful.

Researchers, Educators, and Activists

Ned Hallowell: ADHD

Edward Hallowell—or Ned, as he is popularly known throughout the field—is a practicing clinician and prolific author on ADHD and many other related topics. I have seen him speak many times, including two presentations he has given for PEN. Hallowell is one of the most positive contributors to the body of information about ADHD, which he often calls a gift. I have travelled far and wide to hear him speak, as the experience is always so uplifting and hopeful, replete with examples of famous people with ADHD. For a quick review of upbeat and practical information about dyslexia and ADHD, watch one of his YouTube presentations (https://www.youtube.com/user/NedHallowell).

During the past 10 years, Hallowell has opened Hallowell Centers in Boston, New York City, Palo Alto, San Francisco, and Seattle. Hallowell also wrote a popular illustrated book on parenting kids with ADHD, *A Walk in the Rain With a Brain*. Visit his website at https://www.drhallowell.com.

Robert Brooks: Parenting Best Practices

Bob Brooks is a veteran child psychologist who is also in private practice, giving positive and practical advice to parents and teachers about how to bring out the best in their kids, whether they have learning differences or not (Brooks & Goldstein, 2004).

Inspiring, warm, and experienced, with more than 30 years dealing with kids of all kinds, Brooks is like a personal experienced psychologist who has only your and your child's best interest at heart. For a quick introduction, read his regularly updated blog with the latest findings from a variety of researchers and psychologists at https://www.drrobertbrooks.com.

Richard Lavoie: Social-Emotional Issues

Rick Lavoie (2007) trained in a residential facility for kids with learning difficulties for more than 30 years and has become required reading or listening for any parent whose child is struggling in school. With his long history of hands-on experience with troubled and different kids, Rick can make a listener understand in an hour what it might take years to discover about dealing with the social-emotional fallout, like anxiety, depression, and sometimes even self-harm, that occurs when a child is left to struggle too long with no help or change for the better in the situation.

Rick has written a number of best-selling books on parenting the different kid. He has also created many easy-to-absorb videos for parents. For a quick look at one of his best analogies, watch "When the Chips Are Down With Rick Lavoie" (https://www.youtube.com/watch?v=78bwTPU CBsE) or visit his website at https://www.ricklavoie.com.

Jenifer Fox: Knowing Your Child's Strengths

Jenifer Fox wrote *Your Child's Strengths* in 2008, when she was still head of the prestigious Purnell School. The idea of a school focused on developing strengths and affinities was still quite revolutionary at the time. Her book about how to discover, develop, and use strengths is another guide for parents to use in purposely noticing and focusing on their kids' strengths as a balance to the deficit-based language used in many school reports.

Your Child's Strengths (Fox, 2008) is a helpful book to use with your child in identifying their jagged profile. Every single person has strengths, and Fox divided them into three different categories: activity strengths, relationship strengths, and learning strengths. The book shares how to talk to your child about using their talents to build strategies and workarounds for any challenges. Fox's website is https://www.jeniferfox.com.

Lea Waters: The Strength Switch

The Strength Switch by Lea Waters (2017) shows how to actually develop the talents and affinities that children exhibit along with their challenges. This book is a breath of fresh air and a much-needed tool for every parent (particularly of a child with a learning difference) who is tired of the deficit-based language used in their children's school conferences. Waters, who has a Ph.D. in the field of positive psychology, presents a systematic way to identify and develop children's strengths. (If this book had existed back in 2003, it would have served as the bible for PEN's founders.)

Waters (2017) defined a strength as more than just a "flair." A strength, according to her definition, has three distinct qualities: performance (your child excels at it), energy that your child derives from it, and high use (it is an activity of choice more often than not). In other words, a strength needs to be nurtured, as it may lead your child to their future career or passion. With this approach, parents can watch their children's attitudes become more positive as they become empowered to follow their interests and joyful activities.

A collection of Waters's talks can be found at https://www.leawaters. com/videos.html.

Angela Duckworth: Perseverance and Passion

Grit by Angela Duckworth (2016) models how parents should think about goals for kids who may seem like square pegs in round holes at school. For those who have ushered their kids through the learning differences journey and watched them develop the fortitude to get up every day to go to school, this book—which became an instant *New York Times* bestseller—is a welcome body of research.

In the preface of her book, Duckworth (2016) shared that her father told her numerous times while she was growing up, "You are no genius" (p. xiii). This comment drove her to constantly question, first in herself and then in those around her, what leads people to be successful. Her quest for an answer led her to Ivy League schools, a variety of jobs ranging from consulting to teaching, and finally to psychology, in which she obtained a Ph.D. Her studies and research over the years answered the question "What leads to success?" with good news for kids who learn differently: Most success is gained not through genius or talent, but through perseverance and passion—something that many, if not most, successful kids with learning differences have developed naturally over the years of their struggles.

Carol Dweck: Growth Mindset

Dweck's (2006/2016) *Mindset* is perhaps the best place to start understanding a child who seems to learn in a different way. If you, like me, once thought that your child's learning difference negated any dreams of success, you need to read Dweck's seminal work. This book is a game changer in understanding how to break old mindsets and learn how to parent differently for the different child. It continues to educate teachers and parents to shed rigid views of what constitutes talent and success.

Every parent should read *Mindset* to give their child the best shot at developing innate talents and interests. You can also watch Dweck's (2014)

TED Talk "The Power of Believing That You Can Improve" at https://www.ted. com/talks/carol_dweck_the_power_of_believing_that_you_can_improve.

Todd Rose: The Revolutionary Square Peg

Todd Rose's (2013) first book, *The Square Peg: My Story and What It Means for Raising Innovators, Visionaries, and Out-of-the-Box-Thinkers*, is an autobiographical account of his own journey from angry misfit to visionary thinker. It is a rich source of hope to anyone who knows a struggling child.

Rose was a frustrated student in early elementary school, where his energy, impulsiveness, and boredom often led to bad behavior and punishments. After dropping out of high school with a .9 GPA, he found his way to college and then graduate school at Harvard University, where he became the head of Mind, Brain, and Education in the Graduate School of Education.

His second book, *The End of Average: How We Succeed in a World That Values Sameness* (Rose, 2016), offered a scientific argument for busting the myth that there is such a thing as an average human, against whom each of us should be measured and graded. It details why school performance is so unpredictable for nontraditional thinkers and outlines Rose's Science of Individuality with its three distinct concepts for analyzing the abilities of a human being. Context, jagged profile, and multiple pathways are identified and explained as ways in which to understand the strengths and challenges any individual brings to a place of learning or work. I have given out hundreds of copies of this book to parents and teachers alike to explain the main problem with schools and what kids face in trying to develop their talents in them.

For a quick introduction to Rose's viewpoint, see his TEDx Talk, "The Myth of Average" (https://www.youtube.com/watch?v=4eBmyttcfU4), or visit his website (https://populace.org).

Organizations

Understood

Parents who have not faced learning challenges can have difficulty understanding their children's experience during a typical school day. Parents of every child should spend some time on the website of the nonprofit organization Understood (https://www.understood.org/en). Although Understood does use disability language on its site, there are also some very useful resources. My favorite by far is "Through Your Child's Eyes" (https://www.understood.org/en/through-your-childs-eyes), which uses customized information from you to simulate your child's learning or attention issues. Through a series of activities that you must try to perform with a learning difference affecting your abilities, you will see firsthand how necessary classroom accommodations can be.

The website also features a series of free webinars with experts who can talk about anything from reading and writing issues, to your child's rights within the IEP (the document that every public school creates for kids with specialized learning needs), to how to cope with family gatherings if your child has ADHD. Understood also provides a checklist of signs and symptoms to look out for in a variety of learning challenges.

Children's Health Council

Children's Health Council (CHC; https://www.chconline.org) offers advice on a variety of learning differences and how to spot them. CHC can guide parents to courses, outpatient treatment centers, therapists, and specialist schools. It offers guidance, courses, and therapies for kids with learning differences, ADHD, anxiety, depression, and ASD. In 2018, CHC acquired Parents Education Network (PEN), the organization I cofounded in 2003. CHC continues to organize the annual EdRev Expo, started by PEN in 2009. EdRev (https://www.edrevsf.org) is the only event of its kind that brings together the whole community—students, parents, educators, and professionals—to share experiences and resources, and make new connections.

Eye To Eye

Eye to Eye (https://eyetoeyenational.org) was founded by Jonathan Mooney (Mooney & Cole, 2000) and David Flink (2014), two classmates with ADHD and dyslexia who met at Brown University. They had the idea that young people like them needed a community of their own to empower them. Their idea was to offer one-on-one tutoring services, setting up college students with learning differences as tutors for struggling young students from surrounding elementary schools. When they saw what a success it was for both the older and younger students, they founded a nonprofit organization, now called Eye to Eye, which has been run by Flink and his own team for more than 20 years. Under Flink's management, the vision has grown into a national organization. Eye to Eye uses a well-developed, tested art curriculum for its meetings between mentors and younger kids. Eye to Eye chapters now exist at more than 60 college campuses throughout the country. This organization has become an effective and popular empowerment group for young adults who learn differently.

In 2014, Flink published *Thinking Differently: An Inspiring Guide for Parents of Children With Learning Disabilities*. I recommend this book for anyone who needs step-by-step instructions on how to work with schools on getting accommodations for kids with dyslexia and ADHD.

Further Reading

Barringer, M.-D., Pohlman, C., & Robinson, M. (2010). *Schools for all kinds of minds: Boosting student success by embracing learning variation.* Jossey-Bass.

Baum, S. M., Schader, R. M., & Owen, S. V. (2017). *To be gifted and learning disabled: Strength-based strategies for helping twice-exceptional students with LD, ADHD, ASD, and more* (3rd ed.). Prufrock Press.

Brock, A., & Hundley, H. (2016). *The growth mindset coach: A teacher's month-by-month handbook for empowering students to achieve.* Ulysses Press.

Brown, T. (2014). *Smart but stuck: Emotions in teens and adults with ADHD.* Jossey-Bass.

Brown, T. E. (2005). *Attention deficit disorder: The unfocused mind in children and adults.* Yale University Press.

Davis, R. (with Braun, E.). (2010). *The gift of dyslexia: Why some of the smartest people can't read . . . and how they can learn* (Updated ed.). Perigree Books.

Goldberg, E. (2009). *The new executive brain: Frontal lobes in a complex world*. Oxford University Press.

Grandin, T., & Duffy, K. (2008). *Developing talents: Careers for individuals with Asperger syndrome and high-functioning autism*. Autism Asperger Publishing Co.

Greene, R. W. (2016). *Raising human beings: Creating a collaborative partnership with your child*. Scribner.

Kaufman, S. B. (2013). *Ungifted: Intelligence redefined. The truth about talent, practice, creativity, and the many paths to greatness*. Basic Books.

Kennedy, D., & Banks, R. (with Grandin, T.). (2011). *Bright not broken: Gifted kids, ADHD, and autism*. Jossey-Bass.

Levine, M. (2002). *A mind at a time: American's top learning expert shows how every child can succeed*. Simon & Schuster.

Levine, M. (2003). *The myth of laziness: America's top learning experts shows how kids—and parents—can become more productive*. Simon & Schuster.

Medina, J. (2014). *Brain rules: 12 principles for surviving and thriving at work, home, and school* (2nd ed.). Pear Press.

Miller, L. (2014). *Sensational kids: Hope and help for children with sensory processing disorder (SPD)* (Rev. ed.). Perigree Books.

Reckmeyer, M. (with Robison, J.). (2016). *Strengths based parenting: Developing your children's innate talents*. Gallup Press.

Rose, T., & Ogas, O. (2018). *Dark horse: Achieving success through the pursuit of fulfillment*. HarperOne.

References

Achor, S. (2010). *The happiness advantage: How a positive brain fuels success in work and life*. Currency.

Ahuja, A. (2014). *Autism makes a happier Silicon Valley*. Financial Times.

All Kinds of Minds. (2019). *Spark the learning revolution*. https://www.allkindsofminds.org/spark-the-learning-revolution

Americans With Disabilities Act of 1990, 42 U.S.C. § 12102 *et seq.* (1990). https://www.ada.gov/pubs/adastatute08.htm

Baer, D. (2015). *Peter Thiel: Asperger's can be a big advantage in Silicon Valley*. Business Insider. https://www.businessinsider.com/peter-thiel-aspergers-is-an-advantage-2015-4

Bavas, J. (2015). *Young adults with autism get employment boost through new program with Hewlett-Packard*. ABC News. https://www.abc.net.au/news/2015-12-03/people-with-autism-given-job-opportunities-with-hewlett-packard/6999510

Belanger, L. (2017). *Those with ADHD might make better entrepreneurs. Here's why*. Entrepreneur. https://www.entrepreneur.com/article/286808

Brooks, R. (2014). The power of parenting. In S. Goldstein & R. Brooks (Eds.), *Handbook of resilience in children* (pp. 443–458). Springer.

Brooks, R., & Goldstein, S. (2004). *The power of resilience: Achieving balance, confidence, and personal strength in your life.* McGraw-Hill.

Cook, G. (2012). *The autism advantage.* The New York Times. https://www.nytimes.com/2012/12/02/magazine/the-autism-advantage.html

Duckworth, A. (2016). *Grit: The power of passion and perseverance.* Scribner.

Dweck, C. S. (2014). *The power of believing that you can improve* [Video]. TED Conferences. https://www.ted.com/talks/carol_dweck_the_power_of_believing_that_you_can_improve

Dweck, C. S. (2015). *Carol Dweck revisits the 'growth mindset.'* Education Week. https://www.edweek.org/ew/articles/2015/09/23/carol-dweck-revisits-the-growth-mindset.html

Dweck, C. S. (2016). *Mindset: The new psychology of success.* Ballantine Books. (Original work published 2006)

Eide, B., & Eide, F. (2011). *The dyslexic advantage: Unlocking the hidden potential of the dyslexic brain.* Plume.

Flink, D. (2014). *Thinking differently: An inspiring guide for parents of children with learning disabilities.* HarperCollins.

Fox, J. (2008). *Your child's strengths: Discover them, develop them, use them.* Penguin Group.

Gardner, H. (2011). *Frames of mind: The theory of multiple intelligences.* Basic Books. (Original work published 1983)

Gilman, L. (2018). *How to succeed in business with ADHD.* ADDitude. https://www.additudemag.com/adhd-entrepreneur-stories-jetblue-kinkos-jupitermedia

The Gow School. (n.d.). *4 people you didn't know were dyslexic.* https://www.gow.org/admissions/blog/4-people-you-didnt-know-were-dyslexic

Grandin, T. (2015). *Parenting different-thinking kids* [Presentation]. Bridges Academy, Studio City, CA, United States.

Hallowell, E. M., & Ratey, J. J. (2011). *Driven to distraction: Recognizing and coping with attention deficit disorder from childhood through adulthood* (Rev. ed.). Anchor Books.

Howlin, P., Goode, S., Hutton, J., & Rutter, M. (2009). Savant skills in autism: Psychometric approaches and parental reports. *Philosophical Transactions of the Royal Society B, 364*(1522), 1359–1367. https://dx.doi.org/10.1098%2Frstb.2008.0328

Individuals With Disabilities Education Act, 20 U.S.C. §1401 *et seq.* (1990). https://sites.ed.gov/idea/statuteregulations

Irvine, C. I. (2008). *Harry Potter's Daniel Radcliffe has dyspraxia*. The Telegraph. https://www.telegraph.co.uk/news/celebritynews/2573230/Harry-Potters-Daniel-Radcliffe-has-dyspraxia.html

Jackson, M. (2010). *Temple Grandin* [Film]. HBO Films.

Khazan, O. (2015). *Autism's hidden gifts*. The Atlantic. https://www.theatlantic.com/health/archive/2015/09/autism-hidden-advantages/406180

Kirk, S. A. (1963, April 6). *Behavioral diagnosis and remediation of learning disabilities* [Conference session]. Conference on Exploration Into Problems of the Perceptually Handicapped Child, Chicago, IL, United States.

Lavoie, R. (2007). *The motivation breakthrough: 6 secrets to turning on the tuned-out child*. Touchstone.

Masters in Special Education. (2019). *5 historical figures who overcame learning disorders*. https://www.masters-in-special-education.com/lists/5-historical-figures-who-overcame-learning-disorders

Mooney, J., & Cole, D. (2000). *Learning outside the lines: Two Ivy League students with learning disabilities and ADHD give you the tools for academic success and educational revolution*. Fireside.

National Center for Learning Disabilities. (2017). *The state of LD: Understanding the 1 in 5*. https://www.ncld.org/archives/blog/the-state-of-ld-understanding-the-1-in-5

Newsom, G. (with Dickey, L.). (2013). *Citizenville: How to take the town square digital and reinvent government*. Penguin.

Reading Rockets. (2018). *When the chips are down with Rich Lavoie* [Video]. YouTube. https://www.youtube.com/watch?v=78bwTPUCBsE

Rose, T. (2016). *The end of average: How we succeed in a world that values sameness*. HarperCollins.

Rose, T. (with Ellison, K.). (2013). *Square peg: My story and what it means for raising innovators, visionaries, and out-of-the-box thinkers*. Hyperion.

Sellers, P. (2008). *JetBlue founder speaks out about his ADD*. Fortune. https://fortune.com/2008/06/12/jetblue-founder-speaks-out-about-his-add

Shaywitz, S. (2003). *Overcoming dyslexia: A new and complete science-based program for reading problems at any level*. Vintage Books.

Waters, L. (2017). *The strength switch: How the new science of strength-based parenting can help your child and your teen flourish*. Avery.

Yale Center for Dyslexia and Creativity. (2017a). *Gavin Newsom, governor of California*. http://dyslexia.yale.edu/story/gavin-newsom

Yale Center for Dyslexia and Creativity. (2017b). *John Irving, award-winning author and screenwriter.* https://dyslexia.yale.edu/story/john-irving

Yale Center for Dyslexia and Creativity. (2017c). *Richard Rogers, architect.* https://dyslexia.yale.edu/story/richard-rogers

Yale Center for Dyslexia and Creativity. (2017d). *The truth about accommodations.* https://www.dyslexia.yale.edu/advocacy/national-advocacy/the-truth-about-accommodations

Yale Center for Dyslexia and Creativity. (2017e). *Whoopi Goldberg, Academy Award-winning actress.* https://dyslexia.yale.edu/story/whoopi-goldberg

Appendix A
Understanding the Psych-Ed Report

The psychoeducational assessment (psych-ed report) can provide invaluable information about how your child learns. This guide will help you get the most out of your child's assessment and keep the focus on their individual strengths. It will not replace thorough conversations with the evaluator, but it will increase your chances of having useful conversations before, during, and after the assessment. See Chapter 4 for more thorough background on this process.

Thanks to the following people for their expertise in helping to develop this resource:

- Alexis Filippini, Ph.D., Executive Director at Building on the Best, and
- Lisa Nowell, Cofounder and Executive Director of Recess Collective.

Before the Evaluation

A full assessment process is a big commitment and can provide a huge (even overwhelming) amount of information about your child's learning and thinking. A few quiet moments to check in ahead of time can reduce stress and uncertainty.

Check in With Yourself

- What are my goals? What do I hope to get out of this process?
- How am I feeling about this process? Do I need to do work through any feelings of my own so I can be a cheerleader for my child?

Check in With the Evaluator

- Ask your evaluator, "My goals are X, Y, and Z. How would you describe the purpose as you see it?" See if your goals match.
- Ask, "How will you look at my child's emotional state?"
- Share a note such as the following:

> Thank you for starting this evaluation process so we can all work together to help my child succeed at school. If at all possible, we would love it if the evaluation could include some insights into my child's areas of strength and affinity as well as deficits. This could be really helpful to us all as we try to work together to figure out which methods will help my child best. (J. Adams, personal communication, February 2016)

Check in With Your Child

- Talk about strengths and challenges.
- Adapt the following examples based on your child's experiences.
  - I've noticed that _____ comes easily to you. I've also noticed that it's frustrating that _____ does not come so easily, even though you work really hard at it. Have you noticed that too? What else do you think?
  - The work that you're going to do with Dr. _____ will help us understand why some things take so much more work than others, and give us some tips.

During the Evaluation

The assessment process usually takes at least two sittings, and it can be helpful to remind everyone (yourself, the assessor, and your child) to focus on strengths that can be used to help propel your child forward, not just challenges holding them back.

After the Evaluation

The report you receive will include a narrative, a list of scores, and recommendations. It's likely to be dense, technical, long, and overly focused on "deficits." Even after years of reviewing these reports, they can feel overwhelming. Usually, the examiner will give it to you in person and review findings, but it's a lot to absorb at once. Remember that although the report is full of rich information, it is also just a snapshot in time.

Note. You can ask for a digital copy of the report and use computer software to have it read aloud to you.

Analyze Results at Your Own Pace and Time

1. **Notice jaggedness within your child.** Note the extremes (the highest and lowest scores), and especially the widest gaps.
2. **Be sure that you are clear about what each area fundamentally means for your child's day-to-day life.** Ask the evaluator:
   - What does this _____ (skill/area) allow my child to do?
   - How does _____ get in the way of my child's performance?
   - How do these different areas interact or influence each other? Are some affecting the others?
   - Is there a core strength/challenge that, if addressed, would impact multiple areas?
   - What are some "easy wins" that I can address quickly and easily?
   - Milestones and mini-milestones: How do I know when interventions at home or at school are helping? What are some incremental changes I could be watching for?

3. **Note intersections of strengths and challenges.** Are there strengths that might be masking a challenge, or challenges hiding a strength? Consider the following:
   - the situations in which your child will likely do best,
   - the situations in which your child will likely struggle,
   - key strengths your child can lean on,
   - key weaknesses to support, and
   - interests to develop.

4. **Create a visual.** Completing a T-Chart of strengths and challenges is one way to do this.

Sample T-Chart of Strengths and Challenges for Sam, Age 6

Strengths	Challenges
• Large vocabulary; strong understanding of spoken language • Advanced understanding and use of academic language • Uses language to work through and solve problems • Easily makes inferences when hearing information • Strong social skills; communicates well with peers and adults	• Processing speed is slow, especially relative to language skills, so he seems slow to take in information, absorb, and respond to it • Holding on to multiple pieces of information, or multiple steps, is challenging, and he may "lose the thread" • Stays focused for only a few minutes at a time • Reading is laborious and inaccurate, even on books that are below his grade level

Notes on How to Use Strengths
Sam understands and uses oral language very well, so he learns a lot from conversations in class or from listening to adults. While Sam is building his reading skills, he may be reading below-grade-level books. To continue to learn age-appropriate or advanced vocabulary and concepts, he should be exposed to spoken language. Authentic opportunities, like speeches or debates, will give him the most meaningful opportunities to use these skills, but as he gets older, audiobooks and text-to-speech will be extremely helpful for making sure his verbal abilities continue to develop.

Appendix B
Sample Psych-Ed Report

The following sample report is similar to psychological evaluation reports that you might receive about your child. As you review the text, pay attention to the underlined sections in particular. These are areas that will be helpful in guiding the student, Sam, and tapping into his strengths to support areas of challenge.

Thanks to the following people for their expertise in helping to develop this resource:

- Ramsey Khasho, Psy.D., Chief Clinical Officer at Children's Health Council, and
- Vivian Keil, Ph.D., Clinical Director at Children's Health Council.

SAMPLE NEUROPSYCHOLOGICAL EVALUATION REPORT

Name: Sam Taylor   **Parents:**   Mary and Jim Taylor
Birth Date: June 30, 2012   **Address:**
Current Age: 6 years   **Parents' Phone:**
School, Grade: First   **Date of Report:** June 30, 2018

Evaluation Dates: February 2 and 9, 2018

Relevant Background Information

Reason for Referral
This section should be checked for accuracy. Incorrect information could result in a misinterpretation of results.

Sam is a 6-year-old boy referred to Children's Health Council (CHC) for an evaluation by his parents. They would like to know what is preventing Sam from being successful in the classroom environment. They feel that there is a large gap between his intelligence and how he performs in the classroom.

Sam's parents reported that he is impulsive and has a low frustration tolerance. He is easily annoyed and can be quick to anger. He tries to avoid all tasks he finds undesirable, and because he has always been a good negotiator, he is often successful in his approach. His parents wonder if his avoidance is due to an underlying learning disability or whether it is more of a behavioral problem or related to his impulsivity. He resists all academic tasks, but especially reading.

In addition to the concerns around his behavior and learning, his parents reported that Sam is becoming increasingly self-critical. They feel that he is losing confidence and are concerned about his self-esteem.

As a result of these questions and concerns, Sam's parents requested the current neuropsychological evaluation. They would like to better understand their son's strengths and weaknesses so that they can work with him more effectively and also help him feel better about himself.

Findings from this evaluation will assist his parents in understanding Sam's neuropsychological profile and academic skills, as well as in gaining recommendations to improve his overall functioning. The results of this evaluation will presumably be used for educational and treatment planning. The evaluation process consisted of formal, structured examination procedures as well as clinical interviews, school observations, behavioral observations, and a review of records.

History

Developmental History: Sam's mother received regular prenatal care and was healthy throughout the pregnancy. Sam was born full-term at a weight of 7 pounds, 4 ounces via vaginal delivery. He did not have any difficulty breathing or crying at birth. Sam and his mother were discharged home from the hospital after 2 days without any significant medical complications.

Mrs. Taylor described Sam as a happy baby with an overall good temperament. He enjoyed being held as an infant. He ate well and gained weight steadily. His sleep patterns were described as normal. There were no medical concerns when he was an infant.

Sam's parents reported that he reached his early developmental milestones at an average age. They did not become concerned with Sam's development until he was in preschool. He showed signs of fine motor weakness, and he resisted any type of schoolwork.

Medical History: Sam is a healthy young boy who has been sick an average amount in his life. He has never had significant illnesses or head injuries. Sam does not have any vision or hearing impairments. He does not take any medications. Sam sees a pediatrician regularly for his wellness checks.

Academic History: Sam is currently in the first grade. His parents feel that he has a good relationship with his teacher. His academic strength is math, whereas he struggles much more with reading and writing. Sam's parents reported that when he is reading, he still has to sound out each letter.

Sam's teacher stated that he is most concerned about Sam's behavioral functioning, specifically his impulsivity, lack of frustration tolerance, and oppositional behaviors. The teacher reported that although Sam can make friends, he struggles to keep them due to his negative attention-seeking behaviors. In addition, his mood swings and difficulty managing his emotions interfere with his functioning both in the classroom and on the playground.

Social History: Sam has always been a social young boy who enjoys engaging with his peers and adults alike. His parents reported that kids tend to be drawn to him, and he is good at initiating social interactions, although he has greater difficulty maintaining relationships. As a result of his impulsive behaviors and emotional and behavioral regulation issues, some kids tend to back away as they get to know him better.

Sam is an active and energetic boy who is physically adept. He enjoys participating in a number of different sports activities for fun, including soccer, baseball, and biking. In addition to sports, Sam likes to watch television and play with remote control cars and video games for fun. He also likes building with LEGO blocks.

Family History: Sam lives with his biological parents and younger sister. His parents reported that he generally gets along well with his sister. Sam's parents acknowledged that Sam's behavior has put strain on the entire household, especially in his relationship with his mother as she tries to help him with school-related tasks.

Sam's parents both received college degrees and are fully employed outside the home. Sam's paternal uncle reportedly was hyperactive as a child and had difficulty in school as a result. A different paternal uncle has dyslexia. Sam's maternal grandmother and mother have anxiety. No other maternal or paternal psychiatric history was reported.

Evaluation and Treatment History: Sam has not been evaluated previously. He has never participated in any treatments or therapies.

Tests Administered

- Wechsler Intelligence Scale for Children Fifth Edition (WISC-V)
- Woodcock-Johnson IV Tests of Cognitive Abilities (WJ IV), selected subtests
- A Developmental Neuropsychological Assessment–Second Edition (NEPSY-II), selected subtests
- Integrated Visual and Auditory (IVA+) Continuous Performance Test
- Wide Range Assessment of Memory and Learning, Second Edition (WRAML-2)

- Wechsler Individual Achievement Test, Third Edition (WIAT-III), selected subtests
- Gray Oral Reading Test, Fifth Edition (GORT-5), Form A
- Jordan Left-Right Reversal Test, Third Edition (Jordan-3)
- Test of Orthographic Competence (TOC)
- Test of Word Reading Efficiency (TOWRE), Form A
- Achenbach Child Behavior Checklist (CBCL)
- Achenbach Teacher Report Form (TRF)
- Conners, Third Edition (Conners 3), Parent and Teacher Forms

Behavioral Observations

School Observations

Sam was observed in his first-grade classroom and also during snack and recess. His class has a total of 28 students in it, although most of the core academic instruction takes place in a smaller group of 14 students. There are two teachers who each have a group of 14 students.

The clinician observed Sam when he was in the smaller group of 14 students. During the morning classroom instruction, the teacher was discussing the letter "d," the sounds it makes, and common sight words that begin with the letter. The students all had a worksheet in front of them. When the teacher instructed the students to write their name on the worksheet, Sam appeared to start but did not finish. He got distracted and was leaning back in his chair and fidgeting with his pencil. He flipped the worksheet over to the back side and appeared to be drawing on it, even though the class was clearly working on the front side.

Sam was observed to be off task and frequently impulsive throughout the observation. When the teacher asked questions that required students to raise their hands, he either blurted out an answer without being called on or did not participate because he was playing with something on the desk (e.g., paper, pencil). Although he did not appear to exhibit any behaviors that were intentionally challenging or oppositional in nature, he did require frequent verbal redirections from his teacher to stay on task.

During recess, Sam quickly ate a handful of crackers and then ran out to the grass area. He was pretending to play baseball with three of his male classmates (e.g., pretending to hit, throw, and catch the ball) because they didn't actually have real baseball equipment to play with. Calvin and his peers were interacting nicely, and no conflict was observed. After recess was over, he forgot his snack bag on the playground.

Clinic Observations

Sam presented as a social and engaging boy who was casually dressed and appropriately groomed. His eye contact was good, as was his rapport with the clinician. Sam was alert and oriented to person, place, time, and situation. He was outgoing and talkative, and clearly wanted to connect with the clinician. He answered both open- and closed-ended questions without difficulty. His language was unremarkable in rate, rhythm, prosody, form, and content. Sam's insight and judgment seemed roughly age-appropriate.

During the evaluation, Sam was extremely fidgety, whether it be kicking his feet around, tilting back in his chair, or shifting his position in the chair. He moved around in his chair often and also got out of his chair to walk around the clinician's office. Sam was impulsive in his tendency to blurt out comments and grab objects on the table. Sam was also observed to be inattentive and off task, and he made numerous careless errors on multiple tasks. He was easily distracted by objects in his environment. Fortunately, despite his off-task behaviors, he was generally responsive to redirection.

When on task, Sam's thought process was generally logical and goal-directed. There was no evidence of distortion in thought process or thought content. He did not appear to be internally preoccupied or responding to internal stimuli. Sam denied significant worries and anxiety. When asked about his mood, he said he is usually "happy" and his affect was congruent. He denied thoughts of self-harm or being aggressive to others, past or present.

Throughout the evaluation, Sam was playful and social. Although he was inattentive, impulsive, and distractible, he was responsive to redirection from the clinician. He benefited from breaks from structured tasks, typically every 15 minutes. There was no evidence of any significant emotional or behavioral disturbance that significantly interfered with his performance during this assessment. As a result, the findings of the present evaluation are considered to be a valid and reliable estimate of Sam's current level of functioning.

Evaluation Results

This section gives results in words and percentiles—it should be highlighted and read carefully for overall insights into Sam's learning strengths and weaknesses.

Cognitive Functioning
The processes involved with intelligence, including memory, reasoning, vocabulary, and nonverbal skills, to answer questions and to solve problems.

The Wechsler Intelligence Scale for Children Fifth Edition (WISC-V) provides an estimate of overall intellectual ability, as well as performance in five domains of cognitive functioning: verbal comprehension, visual spatial, fluid reasoning, working memory, and processing speed. Sam's scores among these domains of intellectual ability were highly variable, ranging from the low average to very high range. He earned a Full Scale IQ (FSIQ) of 109, which is in the average range of intellectual functioning. However, given the significant discrepancies among his IQ indices, his FSIQ should not be interpreted in isolation. Rather, individual indices and subtest scores must be examined for a more accurate understanding of his cognitive strengths and weaknesses.

Verbal Comprehension: Sam performed in the very high range on the Verbal Comprehension Index, with his abilities being at the 95th percentile. These language-based subtests assessed his ability to think in words and to apply language skills and verbal information to solve problems. This skillset represents Sam's greatest cognitive strength. His performance was at the 91st percentile on the measure of abstract conceptual reasoning, Similarities. Sam's performance was at the 95th percentile on the vocabulary subtest, a measure of his word knowledge.

Visual Spatial: Sam's performance on the Visual Spatial Index was in the average range, with his visual perceptual abilities and constructional skills being at the 42nd percentile. His performance was at the 50th percentile on the measure of visual spatial analysis and block construction, Block Design. His score was at the 37th percentile on the measure that required him to analyze and synthesize abstract visual information. On this visual puzzles subtest, Sam was asked to view a completed puzzle and then asked to choose three of the response options that would combine to reconstruct the puzzle.

Fluid Reasoning: Sam's performance on the Fluid Reasoning Index was also in the average range, with his score being at the 73rd percentile. This factor assessed his ability to engage in abstract, inductive, and deductive reasoning. These findings indicate that his nonverbal conceptual reasoning skills and visual-spatial abilities are relatively weaker than his superior verbal reasoning abilities. Sam earned a score at the 63rd percentile on the measure of abstract perceptual reasoning. On this matrix reasoning subtest, Sam was asked to identify the missing piece in a colored matrix or visual pattern. Sam's performance was at the 75th percentile on the figure weights subtest, a measure of quantitative and analogical reasoning.

Working Memory: Sam's performance on the Working Memory Index of the WISC-V was in the average range and at the 68th percentile. This index assessed his ability to remember verbally- and visually-presented information, hold it in short-term memory, and manipulate that information to produce some response. Sam's score was strong and at the 75th percentile on the picture span subtest, where he was presented with pictures for 5 seconds and then was asked to identify them from a larger set of pictures. His performance was at the 50th percentile on the digit span subtest that required him to repeat strings of numbers of increasing length—forward, backward, and also in numerical order.

Processing Speed
These tasks measure skills in speed or rate of mental processing and problem solving.

Sam showed a significant weakness in the area of processing speed, and this was seen across multiple measures, with his performance falling well below the expected range. Sam performed in the low average range and at the 9th percentile on the Processing Speed Index of the WISC-V, revealing a significant area of weakness for him. This factor measured his speed of processing simple information and required rapid decision making and motor responses. His score fell at the 16th percentile on the coding subtest, a measure of visuomotor speed and coordination. His performance was at the 9th percentile on the measure of visual scanning and rapid decision making, symbol search.

Sam also completed the processing speed measures from the Woodcock-Johnson Test of Cognitive Abilities (WJ IV). The first, Pair Cancellation, required Sam to scan rows of small repeating pictures of soccer balls, cups, and dogs. He was asked to circle the pairs of pictures each time he saw a ball followed by a dog and had 3 minutes to circle as many as possible. Sam was only able to circle 13 pairs during this time frame. During the administration of this task, Sam announced that he was done after one minute, having completed only half of the first page of pictures. He did continue working after encouragement from the clinician but made comments such as, "Every single row?", "I'm totally tired," and "Must I do it?" Significant prompting was required to have Sam work for the full 3 minutes. During a portion of the time, Sam was coloring in the pictures of the soccer balls. On this measure, Sam performed at the 5th percentile for his age. Although this may be an underrepresentation of how many pairs he could find in 3 minutes with full attention, it illustrates the difficulty Sam experiences with focus and speeded processing.

Sam completed two other processing speed measures from the WJ IV: Letter-Pattern Matching and Number-Pattern Matching. On these two tasks, Sam was asked to find the two identical letters or numbers in a row. For instance, a row might include "L S h L b," and Sam would need to mark the two L's. Again, Sam had 3 minutes to complete each measure. Sam experienced similar difficulty on these two measures as on Pair Cancellation. He required significant prompting to continue and asked many questions during administration that impacted his speed. When marking items, he would occasionally start coloring them in or darkening his lines until prompted to move on. Sam's sustained attention, and ability to maintain a constant speed of processing under time pressure, is significantly impaired. On Letter-Pattern Matching, Sam performed at the 4th percentile and on Number-Pattern Matching, his performance fell below the 1st percentile. Collectively, these measures demonstrate the difficulty that Sam has when asked to keep a steady pace of work, even for just a few minutes.

Attention and Executive Functioning
The ability to sustain attention, self-regulate, self-monitor, inhibit impulsive responding, think flexibly, adapt to the changing demands of the environment, and incorporate feedback into subsequent problem solving.

Sam's attention processes were evaluated using the Auditory Attention and Inhibition subtests of the NEPSY-II. On the Auditory Attention task, he was asked to listen to a list of words and touch the red circle in the stimulus book whenever he heard the word *red*; he was instructed to ignore all other words. This task lasts for approximately 3 minutes. <u>His auditory attention and vigilance on this simple and repetitive task fell below the expected level range, with his performance being at the 5th percentile.</u> Furthermore, he made more omission errors (total omission errors = 11th–25th percentile), commission errors (total commission errors = 6th–10th percentile), and inhibitory errors (total inhibitory errors = 6th–10th percentile) than typical, indicating that he struggles to regulate his attention processes and makes numerous errors. His response pattern revealed significant inattention and impulsivity.

Sam was administered the Inhibition subtest of the NEPSY-II to assess his inhibitory control, cognitive flexibility, and self-monitoring. The first task required him to first name shapes (i.e., circle or square) or the directions of arrows (i.e., up or down). His overall performance was below the expected level and fell at the 2nd percentile. In addition, he completed the task more slowly than typical. He made many more errors than typical (total errors = 2nd–5th percentile), suggesting that attention regulation and self-monitoring are significant areas of weakness for Sam.

On the next task assessing inhibition, he was asked to name the opposite shape (i.e., circle for square and vice versa) or direction (i.e., up for down arrow and vice versa). Sam's overall performance on this task was again below the expected level, as was his error rate (total errors = 2nd–5th percentile), although he was able to complete the task in the amount of time expected. The clinician redirected Sam on multiple occasions to keep going as he tended to stop and get off task. He also exhibited a weakness in working memory as he had difficulty retaining the instructions and at one point forgot the instructions of the Inhibition condition and instead followed the instructions of the Naming condition. Sam's difficulties on this task highlight his weaknesses in a number of areas, including working memory, inattention, impulsivity, and self-monitoring.

Sam's auditory and visual attention skills were assessed using the Integrated Visual and Auditory (IVA+) Continuous Performance Test, which measures his attentional functioning and impulse control. On this repetitive task that lasts approximately 15 minutes, he was asked to attend to a computer screen and click the mouse when he either heard or saw the number 1, and not click the mouse when he heard or saw the number 2. Sam's overall performance was impaired, and he was visibly struggling to keep up with the demands of this task. His Full Scale Attention scale (standard score = 80) fell in the mildly impaired range, indicating that he has significant difficulty sustaining his attention processes, and this was true for both auditory and visual stimuli.

Sam's auditory attention fell in the slightly impaired range, with his performance falling at the 18th percentile. His Auditory Vigilance and Auditory Acuity scores all fell in the severely impaired range, indicating that his general auditory attentional functioning is weak, and this was especially true for low-demand situations. In other words, he had significant problems remaining alert when the targets were less prevalent. Sam's visual attention fell in the mildly to moderately impaired range as his performance was at the 7th percentile. As seen in the auditory modality, he showed weaknesses in visual attention, particularly under low-demand situations, as seen by his Moderately Impaired Visual Vigilance and Visual Acuity scores. Sam's overall pattern of responses on the IVA+ was consistent with a diagnosis of ADHD.

Working Memory, Verbal, and Visual Memory
The retention and recall of verbal and/or visual information over brief intervals (e.g., seconds or minutes) and over longer periods of time.

Auditory/Verbal Memory: On the WRAML-2, Sam's ability to recall verbally presented stories and words was solidly in the average range at the 70th percentile. His performance was in the average range when asked to recall stories and in the high average range when recalling word lists. Sam's ability to recognize the verbal stimuli among distracters after a time delay remained in the average range. Sam had some difficulty with the unstructured nature of story retelling, providing only a general summary until prompted to provide more details. Upon prompting he said, "Like what? About the birthday party and the roller skating?", indicating that he did retain more details about the story than his initial retelling presented. This finding suggests that Sam's performance is likely to improve when tasks have greater structure.

Visual Memory: Sam's ability to recall visual information was relatively weaker and at the 34th percentile, although still in the average range. His memory for picture scenes was much stronger than his memory for designs, with his performance on the latter falling in the borderline range and at the 9th percentile. His ability to recognize the visual stimuli among distracters after a time delay was weaker and fell in the low average range. On the design memory task, Sam was shown simple geometric designs for a few seconds and asked to reproduce them. He frequently did not start scanning the designs right away or spoke to the clinician while looking at the designs. Given the short exposure time on this task, his weaknesses in attention likely had a negative impact on his performance. He reported that this was the hardest of the memory tasks for him.

Academic Functioning

The educational battery addresses the underlying processing skills needed for reading, writing, math, and overall academic achievement. These include phonological processing and the language needed to benefit from school instruction.

Academic Language

Higher level language skills, critical for academic endeavors and school success.

In order to experience success in school, students must have the language skills to understand and learn from verbal information, as well as express their knowledge and demonstrate mastery. Academic language refers to the vocabulary, comprehension, and expression skills necessary to learn and communicate in a school setting. <u>Oral language is an area of particular strength for Sam and represented the highest performance of his academic scores.</u> On the Oral Language Composite of the Wechsler Individual Achievement Test (WIAT-III), <u>Sam performed at the 79th percentile for his age in the high average range.</u>

Sam demonstrated strong listening comprehension throughout testing. He understood the directions for all tasks presented to him and appeared to understand all of the instructions given by the clinician. On the Listening Comprehension portion of the WIAT-III, Sam performed at the 84th percentile overall. His receptive vocabulary was in the average range. Sam's strongest performance was on the Oral Discourse Comprehension subtest. Sam listened to recordings of stories, conversations, and commercials. After each recording was played, he was asked questions about what he had heard. He was only allowed to hear each recording once. Sam was able to answer comprehension questions about passages beyond that expected for his age. Sam performed in the superior range at the 98th percentile.

Expressive language is also an area of strength for Sam. His expressive vocabulary was at the 86th percentile for his age. He performed in the average range on both Oral Word Fluency and Sentence Repetition. Oral Word Fluency asked Sam to provide as many words as possible that fit a category in one minute, and sentence repetition asked him to repeat sentences verbatim. Although Sam performed in the average range, these performances are lower than his other oral language scores. This relatively lower performance is likely due to his challenges with attention and processing speed, rather than a language difficulty. Overall, Sam is a very verbal young man, and oral language is one of his most significant strengths.

Reading
Decoding/sight word reading and text comprehension as well as speed of reading.

Given Sam's strengths in verbal reasoning and oral language, reading should be an academic strength for him. In contrast, Sam's reading scores all fall below the 50th percentile, suggesting that he is experiencing difficulty with reading, particularly given his exceptional verbal reasoning capacity. Sam completed two measures of reading fluency, both the Oral Reading subtest from the WIAT-III and the Gray Oral Reading Test (GORT-5). On both of these measures, Sam demonstrated low average accuracy and significant difficulty with reading rate.

Sam's difficulties with both accuracy and rate when reading stem from multiple processing deficits. First, Sam's slower processing speed impacts his ability to quickly retrieve information, such as words and sounds that letters make. This slows down his reading even when he knows all of the words. Further, Sam has difficulty with reading accuracy, making errors such as reading "deg" for the word *big*. Despite these reading challenges, Sam's strong verbal skills allow him to use context clues to comprehend some of what he is trying to read.

When reading single words, there are several strategies a student can use to determine the word. For instance, a student can use context to guess what the next word might be. Two of the primary strategies used by young students are decoding (sounding the word out based upon the sounds each letter makes) and sight reading (recognizing the entire word as one unit that has been memorized). Sam's decoding skills are in the average range for his age. He completed two measures of single-word decoding that asked him to read nonsense words, such as *mub* and *wep*. As these words are made up, there is no way that Sam can read them from memory and must thus rely on his understanding of the sounds and rules of English. On the first measure, Pseudoword Decoding from the WIAT-III, Sam performed at the 45th percentile. On the second, Phonemic Decoding Efficiency from the Test of Word Reading Efficiency (TOWRE), Sam performed at the 30th percentile. Both of these performances fall within the average range for his age, although clearly below his cognitive potential.

In contrast, Sam experienced more difficulty on single-word reading tasks that required him to read words that he should have memorized and be able to read by sight. He again completed two measures, one on the WIAT-III and one on the TOWRE, to assess this skill. On each of these he performed at the 37th and 16th percentiles, respectively. His performance on the Sight Word Efficiency subtest (TOWRE) falls in the below-average range for his age. He misread *no* as *on*, *as* as *has*, and *book* as *bock*. These errors indicate that Sam has difficulty looking at the distinct visual features of each word and relies too heavily on decoding as a reading strategy.

The Test of Orthographic Competence (TOC) assessed some of the different aspects of orthographic ability that relate to the reading and spelling of sight words. On two measures from this test, Sam performed in the average range for his age at the 63rd percentile. These two measures looked at rule-governed, concrete concepts—Signs and Symbols, as well as Punctuation. The two measures that were more visually based were significantly more difficult for Sam. One, Homophone Choice, asked Sam to select the correct spelling of different words from multiple options. Each spelling option was phonetically accurate but not orthographically (e.g., *whale* vs. *wail* when shown a picture of a whale). On this measure, Sam's performance fell at the 9th percentile for his age. Because Sam relies on the phonetic structure of words, this task was extremely difficult for him as he needed to access his visual memory and the orthographic structure. The most challenging task for Sam was Grapheme Matching, which required him to scan a row of letters, numbers, and symbols and find the two that matched. This task was timed, which is difficult for Sam due to his slow processing speed. Additionally, he made errors by selecting graphemes that were similar but not the same. For instance, he circled a "b" and "p" as the same letter. As the items became two letters in length (e.g., "po" and "op"), Sam was unable to answer any correctly. On this measure Sam performed at the 1st percentile.

Due to Sam's difficulty with several orthographic tasks, as well as his frequent reversals in letters and numbers, he was given the Jordan

Left-Right Reversal Test. This task required him to identify numbers and letters that are in an incorrect orientation. Although Sam was able to identify many of the reversed letters and numbers, he also misidentified a large portion of them as incorrect when they were not. During testing he commented to the clinician, "I never know which way the letters are supposed to go." On this measure Sam performed at the 1st percentile, which is clearly a significant area of weakness for him. It is also important to note that this measure was untimed.

Sam's reading performance is impacted by several processing deficits, including his slow processing speed, low average working memory, weaker visual memory, and orthographic awareness deficits. Together, these create difficulty reading sight words, quickly retrieving labels, and distinguishing the differences between visually similar words and letters. Sam's intact phonological processing skills and his strong verbal reasoning ability allow him to compensate for some of his weaknesses by relying on decoding and context clues when reading. Nevertheless, Sam's reading is below the level expected given his age and cognitive potential.

Written Language
Spelling of individual letters and his name.

At Sam's young age, writing skills are primarily determined by alphabet writing ability, basic spelling, and general knowledge of writing-related information and skills. Overall, writing is an area of average performance for Sam. First, Sam was asked to write as many letters of the alphabet as he could in 30 seconds (Alphabet Writing Fluency—WIAT-III). Sam was able to produce five letters—*c, i, k, l,* and *s*—in lower case. The paper on which he wrote was primary ruled paper with the dotted line through the center. Sam did attend to the lines when writing, and his letters were appropriately sized for the lines available. For this measure, Sam performed in the average range at the 27th percentile compared to students his age.

Sam experienced more success on the spelling subtest of the WIAT-III. The initial items asked Sam to write the letter that made certain sounds (e.g., Write the letter that makes the /d/ sound, as in "dog"). Sam was able to do this with 100% accuracy. When asked to try writing words, he was able to accurately spell the words *cat, in,* and *fix.* On this measure, Sam performed at the 53rd percentile.

Sam does experience difficulty with letter and number formation and frequently produces reversals. As mentioned previously, the TOC measures different aspects of spelling, including conventions, speed, and accuracy. Sam had the most difficulty choosing the correct spelling for different words and matching identical graphemes. This weakness will impact his spelling ability, as he will have difficulty relying on his visual and motor memory when writing. Sam should pair spelling with his strong verbal skills by creating scripts for troublesome words and letters. Overall, Sam possesses many intact written language skills. However, his weaker visual memory and orthographic awareness deficits impact his letter formation and sight word spelling skills.

Math
Early math skills.

Mathematics is an area of mixed performance for Sam. On a measure of Numerical Operations (WIAT-III) Sam was able to answer several questions. He was able to count quantities, identify and circle the numbers out of a mix of numbers and letters, and was able to identify the missing number from the number line 1–10. He missed one early problem due to a number reversal. Sam was also able to correctly answer all of the single-digit addition problems. He was unable to complete any subtraction problems, as he answered them simply by rewriting the initial number. For instance, he wrote $3 - 1 = 3$, and $6 - 2 = 6$. On this pencil and paper math measure, Sam performed at the 27th percentile for his age.

Similarly, Sam performed within the average range on a measure of more applied problem solving (Math Problem Solving, WIAT-III). These questions were presented orally instead of on paper, although they did have a visual complement and could be repeated to Sam. Further, he had an unlimited amount of time to answer. Sam was able to read graphs, complete word problems, identify larger and smaller numbers, and count quantities. He began missing items when asked questions about time, calendars, and coins. On this measure, Sam performed at the 23rd percentile.

Sam also completed two measures of math fluency, which required him to complete as many single-digit arithmetic problems as possible in one minute. On the addition subtest of this measure, Sam performed in the average range at the 58th percentile. He had more difficulty on the subtraction subtest as he was unable to compute the problems, performing at the 13th percentile for his age. This performance reflects his difficulty with subtraction, rather than an underlying math fluency difficulty. To summarize, Sam demonstrates age-appropriate mathematics skills, although he has difficulty completing timed measures and those that require multiple steps.

Emotional and Behavioral Functioning
How children understand and view themselves and others' perceptions of them; how children experience mood and how it affects them; how children regulate their actions.

Sam's overall emotional and behavioral functioning was assessed using the Achenbach Child Behavior Checklist (CBCL), completed by his mother, and Teacher Report Form (TRF), completed by his current teacher. On the CBCL, the responses from his mother produced elevations on the following symptom subscales: Anxious/Depressed (T-score = 78), Rule-Breaking Behavior (T-score = 67), Aggressive Behavior (T-score = 67). In terms of diagnostic subscales, she endorsed elevations on the Affective Problems (T-score = 73), Anxiety Problems (T-score = 70), Attention Deficit/Hyperactivity Problems (T-score = 66), and Oppositional Defiant Problems (T-score = 70) subscales.

Sam's current teacher reported elevations on the following symptom subscales: Anxious/Depressed (T-score = 71), Thought Problems (T-score = 66), Attention Problems (T-score = 69), and Aggressive Behavior (T-score = 80). Her responses produced elevations on the diagnostic subscales for Affective Problems (T-score = 65), Attention Deficit/Hyperactivity Problems (T-score = 70), Oppositional Defiant Problems (T-score = 75), and Conduct Problems (T-score = 68).

Given the concerns regarding Sam's attention processes, his parents and teacher all completed the Conners 3. His father reported significant elevations on the following subscales: Inattention (T-score = 72), Hyperactivity/Impulsivity (T-score = 90), Executive Functioning (T-score = 75), Defiance/Aggression (T-score = 84), and Peer Relations (T-score = 72). His responses produced an elevation on the diagnostic scales for ADHD Predominantly Inattentive Type (T-score = 80), ADHD Predominantly Hyperactive-Impulsive Type (T-score = 86), and Oppositional Defiant Disorder (T-score = 77).

His mother reported significant elevations on the following subscales: Hyperactivity/Impulsivity (T-score = 81), Learning Problems (T-score = 65), Executive Functioning (T-score = 71), and Defiance/Aggression (T-score = 84). Her responses produced an elevation on the diagnostic scales for ADHD Predominantly Inattentive Type (T-score = 68), ADHD Predominantly Hyperactive-Impulsive Type (T-score = 76), and Conduct Disorder (T-score = 66).

His teacher's responses on the Conners 3 produced elevations on the Inattention (T-score = 65), Hyperactivity/Impulsivity (T-score = 83), Defiance/Aggression (T-score = 90), and Peer Relations (T-score = 74). This resulted in significant elevations on the diagnostic scales for ADHD Predominantly Hyperactive-Impulsive Type (T-score = 84), Conduct Disorder (T-score = 86), and Oppositional Defiant Disorder (T-score = 90).

Summary and Integrated Diagnostic Formulation

This section provides an overall verbal impression of Sam's jagged profile.

Sam is a talkative and social 6-year-old boy who was evaluated due to concerns with regard to his avoidance behaviors, impulsivity, and difficulty being successful in the classroom environment. Throughout the evaluation, Sam was distractible and needed frequent breaks and regular redirection to sustain his attention. He was generally responsive to redirection and put forth adequate effort. Thus, the results from the current multidisciplinary evaluation are considered to be a valid and reliable estimate of Sam's current level of functioning.

The findings from this evaluation indicate that Sam's neurocognitive profile is highly variable, with clear areas of strength and weakness. His verbal reasoning abilities represent a significant strength for him, as his abilities are in the very high range. Sam's nonverbal reasoning abilities and visual-spatial skills are relatively weaker than his verbal reasoning abilities, although they are still in the average range. This discrepancy between his verbal and nonverbal reasoning abilities suggests that language-based subjects, such as reading, should be relatively easier than more visually-based subjects, such as mathematics. However, this is not the case for Sam, as he has significant processing and learning differences that are interfering with his ability to reach his cognitive potential.

Sam's processing speed is one of his greatest areas of weakness. His processing speed with even simple tasks is significantly below average.

This undoubtedly impacts all aspects of learning and creates a tremendous amount of frustration for him. Because Sam's cognitive efficiency, or the rate at which he can process information, is much slower than that of his peers, he will need academic accommodations such as extra time on tests and assignments.

Sam also has a weakness in working memory in that he has difficulty mentally "holding onto" multiple pieces of information. Although his performance on the simpler working memory tasks of the WISC-V was average, he was forgetful on more complex tasks, and repetition of instructions was needed on multiple occasions. Because Sam's working memory is weaker than that of his same-age peers, if he is told to complete X, Y, and Z, he may complete one or even two tasks, but he is unlikely to complete all three of them successfully; he cannot maintain all of the instructions online and available in his mind. Given this weakness, it is recommended that adults in Sam's life provide him with simplified instructions one at a time, and also provide accompanying visual support rather than giving him complex or multistep instructions.

Weaknesses in working memory are often seen among individuals with attentional deficits. Indeed, on standardized tests of attention and executive functioning, Sam exhibited significant weaknesses in the areas of inattention, impulsivity, and attention regulation. His overall performance tended to be highly inconsistent and inaccurate, indicating that Sam has difficulty regulating and sustaining his attention processes. He made numerous errors across a number of tasks, indicating that he has a weakness in inhibition and self-monitoring. Furthermore, school observations and behavior observations made during the evaluation indicate that he is impulsive, distractible, and inattentive, even when he has one-to-one attention. In addition to these behavioral observations and Sam's performance on standardized tests, his parents and teacher all reported significant symptoms of inattention, hyperactivity, and impulsivity. All of these data and observations indicate that he meets the diagnostic criteria for Attention Deficit/Hyperactivity Disorder (ADHD), Combined Type.

In addition to ADHD, Sam has a specific learning disability in reading that is interfering with his ability to reach his full potential. Results from the educational evaluation indicate that Sam's oral language skills are a tremendous strength. Despite this strength, however, he does demonstrate significant discrepancies in his reading performance. Although Sam's phonological processing is age-appropriate and his oral comprehension is strong, he has difficulty with the visual aspects of reading, including letter discrimination, sight word reading, and some spelling. These difficulties are due to his orthographic awareness deficits and weaker visual memory skills. They are further impacted by his slow processing speed and weaker working memory, which make it difficult for him to process information quickly and efficiently. When writing, Sam frequently reverses letters and numbers, and has difficulty spelling words from memory, relying solely on phonetic knowledge. Overall, he demonstrates reading skills that are significantly discrepant from his expected achievement and cognitive ability, which is due to several processing deficits. These findings indicate that Sam meets the criteria for a specific learning disorder in reading, frequently referred to as dyslexia.

Sam's emotional functioning also warrants some discussion, as it undoubtedly contributes to some of his difficulties in the classroom. He is a bright boy with slow processing speed and a specific learning disability that makes it very challenging for him to be successful in the classroom. This asynchrony in his development has created a great deal of internal frustration and insecurity for Sam, which contributes to his avoidance behaviors and negative attention-seeking behaviors. Although some of his negative self-statements, such as "I'm dumb," may be attention-seeking at times, these critical comments also seem to reflect his true insecurity and negative self-esteem. Once Sam experiences greater success in the classroom, hopefully he will feel more capable, and his self-esteem will improve. It is recommended that his parents continue to monitor his emotional functioning closely; should it not improve, and certainly if it worsens, they are encouraged to reach out to this clinician or another mental health professional to determine the most appropriate next steps.

In summary, Sam is a bright and social young boy who wants to be successful. Although he has weaknesses in his attention and learning in particular, he has numerous strengths. His verbal reasoning is advanced, and his oral language and verbal memory are solid. Sam's communication skills are clearly an asset to be utilized in his learning and intervention strategies. He is socially motivated and has a positive relationship with his teacher. In addition to Sam's individual strengths, his parents are committed to supporting their son as he strives to reach his full potential. All of these strengths combined will help Sam be more successful in his endeavors. The following specific recommendations are offered to assist Sam, his family, and his teachers in addressing his areas of weakness.

Diagnoses (DSM-5 and ICD-10)

Results indicate that Sam meets criteria for the following diagnoses, according to the *Diagnostic and Statistical Manual of Mental Disorders* (5th ed.) and the *International Classification of Diseases* (10th ed.):

- ADHD, Combined Type (314.01)
- Specific Learning Disorder with Impairment in Reading (315.00)

Recommendations

Recommendations should be discussed with Sam's teacher(s) and school learning specialist, as well as his tutor if he has one. This list can be overwhelming, so it is recommended that parents and school personnel try a few recommendations at a time and ask Sam what he thinks would help him.

1. It is recommended that this evaluation team meet with Sam's educational team at his school to discuss the central findings and recommendations from the current multidisciplinary evaluation so that Sam's teachers and relevant school personnel can better understand his cognitive strengths and weaknesses and accommodate his individual needs.
2. It is recommended that Sam's parents consider a medication consultation with a child and adolescent psychiatrist. Sam is a capable young boy who wants to do well. His symptoms of inattention and impulsivity are clearly interfering with his ability to reach his full potential at home and in school. Medication can be helpful in improving attention processes and reducing hyperactivity and impulsivity.
3. Given Sam's slow processing, attention weaknesses, and learning difference in reading, it is recommended that his parents consider smaller schools that focus on language-based learning differences.
4. It is recommended that Sam work with a reading specialist to help remediate his reading. He should work with specialists who are trained in multisensory learning methodologies, such as Orton-Gillingham, Slingerland Approach.
5. Sam exhibits many challenging behaviors, such as impulsivity, defiance, noncompliance, and aggression. His parents are encour-

aged to consider working with behavioral specialist who can help them create a behavioral system of rewards and consequences that effectively reduces these behaviors.

6.   Given that Sam can be inattentive and distractible, it is recommended that he be given preferred seating toward the front and center of the classroom and in a relatively quiet classroom location (e.g., away from the main door, close to the teacher, away from chatty students).

7.   It is recommended that Sam take routine and frequent breaks during extended work and study periods so as to maximize his attention span. He should be given frequent movement breaks throughout the school day. For example, after working for 15 minutes, he could be allowed to get a drink of water, help the teachers distribute papers, or run a lap outside before sitting down to work for another 15 minutes.

8.   If it would be helpful, Sam should be allowed to take tests in a separate quiet room with limited distractions. To reduce his distractibility, it may be helpful for him to wear earphones when appropriate in the classroom. Standing folders up on his desk to create a study carrel may also be beneficial.

9.   To reduce off-task behaviors, a silent cue could be set up between Sam and his teacher. For example, his teacher could set up a signal with Sam, such as gently squeezing or tapping his shoulder, that only the two of them know, and the teacher could send the signal to him every time that he notices that Sam is off task. This silent cue may allow Sam to become more aware of his behavior while not embarrassing him in front of his classmates. Verbal prompts and reminders (e.g., "Sam, please pay attention") often have the unintended consequence of embarrassing the student.

10.   In addition to verbal prompting, Sam may benefit more from visual cues and aids when teaching him and redirecting his attention. For example, rather than relying on only verbal prompts to transition Sam to the next activity, it may be helpful for his parents and teachers to use visual schedules to help keep him on task. A schedule of his daily classroom activities could be posted to his desk at school. Thus, when it is time for his teachers to remind him to take out his reading book, he will also have the visual aid in front of him to help remind him what he needs to do next.

11. Provide Sam with easily accessible visual references of the alphabet and numbers so he can check on their sequence and orientation. Taping strips of letters and numbers to his desk at school and at home will provide immediate access to this information. Creating verbalizations that help him remember orientation of letters and numbers is helpful as well (e.g., "b is a bat and then a ball" and "d is a doughnut and a door" paired with a visual referent).

12. Given Sam's slow processing speed, it should be expected that his entire learning process will progress more slowly than that of most of his peers. He needs additional time to learn, or encode, new information, and he needs more time to remember, or recall, information from his memory. In addition, his work output is slow so he needs additional time to complete tests and assignments.

13. Sam's working memory skills represent an area of weakness for him, so he has difficulty mentally holding onto information that is presented to him. It is recommended that his parents and teachers give him only one instruction at a time. It should be expected that he will need repetition of instructions.

14. Learning how to spell can be made more fun by having Sam arrange magnetic letters on his fridge or use bath crayons to spell words in the shower or bath. He should say the name of the letters out loud as he spells in order to access auditory, visual, and kinesthetic feedback at the same time. After he has learned his list of spelling words, parents can ask him to spell each word in reverse. This will assess his ability to hold onto the sequence of letters in his working memory.

15. Sam should be encouraged to use color-coding to help him attend to math operation signs (e.g., green for addition, red for subtraction). He can also try color-coding his sentences (e.g., green for a capital letter at the start of a sentence, red for punctuation at the end of a sentence).

16. The following are additional recommendations for Sam's dyslexia:
    - Assign fewer spelling words to study for a weekly test, gradually increasing the number of words Sam should know how to spell as the year progresses.
    - No student should grade Sam's written work.
    - Provide extended time on tests.
    - Consider reduced homework or limit the time Sam is required to spend each night on homework. If he cannot get through

the entire homework assignment, prioritize the workload for him.

- Access Bookshare (https://www.bookshare.org/cms) or Learning Ally (https://learningally.org) for text-to-speech support. Bookshare provides test-to-speech support in all assigned textbooks at no cost to all eligible students with reading differences.

- Support note-taking by allowing Sam to use a copy of his teacher's notes or notes from a classmate.

- Homework assignments should be prewritten for Sam; he should not be expected to quickly and accurately copy assignments written on the board.

- Consider oral testing when appropriate.

- Allow Sam access to a reader on classroom and standardized tests as needed.

- Do not penalize for spelling errors on assignments that are graded on the quality of his ideas and on how he expresses himself in print.

- Do not demand that he read out loud in class or partake in spelling bees.

- Provide Sam with extra visual structure on worksheets and assignments. For example, arrange problems in numbered boxes or columns. His worksheets and assignments should include enlarged font and fewer text or equations on any one worksheet. This accommodation should be available to Sam during classroom tests as well.

- Sam should be encouraged to learn to type and use speech-to-text technology when he is older.

- In later grades, Sam should be allowed to write classroom and standardized tests on a computer, with access to spell- and grammar-check. Grammarly software is more effective at checking errors in spelling and grammar than the standard programs installed in word programs.

17. It may be helpful for Sam's parents to utilize lists even in everyday, nonacademic tasks, such as grocery shopping. For example, Sam can help make a list of what groceries are needed and can also help cross them off. If Sam becomes accustomed to using lists

effectively in such real-life situations, this may help improve his working memory and planning skills.

18. Sam would benefit from having a quiet and organized study area to complete his schoolwork that is free from distractions, such as television or video games. He should become accustomed to working in this study area and establish a daily study schedule to help keep him focused.

19. Schedules and lists will help Sam organize and keep track of familiar routines and assignments. Breaking up the steps and having Sam check them off as he completes them will allow him to find his place if he becomes off task, and know where to start and end.

20. Sam's parents may find the following books helpful:
    - *Taking Charge of ADHD: The Complete, Authoritative Guide for Parents* (3rd ed.) by Russell Barkley.
    - *Overcoming Dyslexia* by Sally Shaywitz.
    - *Learning Outside the Lines* by Jonathon Mooney and David Cole. This book is a personal account of growing up with ADHD and dyslexia and becoming successful despite these learning differences.
    - *Late, Lost, and Unprepared: A Parents' Guide to Helping Children with Executive Functioning* by Joyce Cooper-Kahn and Laurie Dietzel. This book includes useful strategies regarding how to provide greater organization and structure in the home.

21. Sam's parents may be interested in exploring the following online resources:
    - Children and Adults With ADHD (CHADD; https://chadd.org)
    - Attention Deficit Disorder Association (ADDA; https://add.org)
    - The International Dyslexia Association (IDA; https://dyslexiaida.org)
    - Understood (https://www.understood.org/en)

22. Frequent communication and coordination of care between Sam's parents and teachers and other treatment providers (e.g., therapists, physicians, tutors) will be crucial in helping him achieve his full potential.

Evaluation Scores

Terms Used in Measures of Performance

Tests of knowledge or performance compare a child's abilities to what would be expected for someone of the same age. Results typically are reported in one or more of the following ways.

Standard Score: This approach converts a child's performance to a scale on which the "average" child will achieve a test score of 10, 50, or 100, depending upon the test. Because individual performance is not that exact, these tests also define a "normal" range of performance, called a *standard deviation*. Knowing a child's standard score, the test average, and the standard deviation, it is easy to see how your child is doing. Unless otherwise noted, standard scores have a mean of 100 and a standard deviation of 15. Standard T-scores have a mean of 50 with a standard deviation of 10. Standard scaled score means are 10 with a standard deviation of 3.

Percentile Rank: Knowledge-based tests often report a child's performance as a ranking. The scale ranges from 1–99, with 99 as the highest. For example, for someone at the 50th percentile, half of those who took the test performed better on the test and half performed worse.

Age Equivalent: This approach is less rigorous than a standard score but may seem more "real life." It estimates how old an average child would need to be to achieve the score one's child did. Thus, if a 6-year-old performed strongly, the age equivalent score might be 8 years 6 months.

Grade Equivalent: Some tests report performance on the basis of the grade at which an average child would be expected to achieve the same result (e.g., a fourth grader with dyslexia might be reading at a second-grade level). Note that grade equivalency scores must be interpreted with some caution as they may not produce actual instructional levels but instead reflect the performance of students who were assessed while in that particular grade.

Score Ranges and Equivalencies

	Deficient	Borderline	Low Average	Average	High Average	Superior	Very Superior
Scaled Score	1–3	4–5	6–7	8–12	13–14	15–16	17+
Standard Score	55–69	70–79	80–89	90–109	110–119	120–129	130+
Percentile	< 1st–2nd	2nd–8th	9th–24th	25th–75th	76th–90th	91st–97th	98th+

Wechsler Intelligence Scale for Children Fifth Edition (WISC-V)

The WISC-V is an individually administered test designed to reflect the intellectual functioning of children ranging in age from 6 years to 16 years, 11 months. The test divides cognitive functioning into five domains—verbal ability, visual perceptual skills, nonverbal reasoning, working memory, and processing speed—and yields the following composite scores: Verbal Comprehension (VCI), Visual Spatial (VSI), Fluid Reasoning (FRI), Working Memory (WMI), Processing Speed (PSI), and Full Scale IQ (the combination of all of the domains measured). The VCI is considered to be a measure of verbal learning, reasoning, and language processing, while the VSI and FRI is considered to be measures of nonverbal, fluid learning, perceptual planning and organization, and visual processing. The WISC-V is highly correlated with academic success, and as such, provides a predictor for academic achievement.

Verbal Comprehension Subtests	Scaled Score	Percentile	
Similarities	14	91st	
Vocabulary	15	95th	
Visual Spatial Subtests	Scaled Score	Percentile	
Block Design	10	50th	
Visual Puzzles	9	37th	
Fluid Reasoning Subtests	Scaled Score	Percentile	
Matrix Reasoning	11	63rd	
Figure Weights	12	75th	

Working Memory Subtests	Scaled Score	Percentile	
Digit Span	10	50th	
Picture Span	12	75th	
Processing Speed Subtests	**Scaled Score**	**Percentile**	
Coding	7	16th	
Symbol Search	6	9th	
Composite Scores	**Standard Score**	**Percentile**	**Description**
Verbal Comprehension Index	124	95th	Very High
Visual Spatial Index	97	42nd	Average
Fluid Reasoning Index	109	73rd	Average
Working Memory Index	107	68th	Average
Processing Speed Index	80	9th	Low Average
Full Scale IQ*	109	73rd	Average

*Cannot be interpreted due to discrepancies among indices

Woodcock-Johnson IV Tests of Cognitive Abilities

This battery of tests measures different aspects of cognitive ability.

	Standard Score	Percentile Rank	Age Equivalent
Processing Speed	**72**	**3**	**4-11**
Pair Cancellation	76	5	4-5
Perceptual Speed	**66**	**1**	**4-9**
Letter-Pattern Matching	74	4	5-2
Number-Pattern Matching	59	0.3	4-5

A Developmental Neuropsychological Assessment–Second Edition (NEPSY-II)

The NEPSY-II consists of a series of neuropsychological subtests that can be used in various combinations to assess neuropsychological development in children ages 3–16.

Auditory Attention/ Response Set	Scaled Score	Percentile	Description
Auditory Attention	5	5th	Below Average
Inhibition	**Scaled Score**	**Percentile**	**Description**
Inhibition-Naming	4	2nd	Below Average
Inhibition-Naming Completion Time	7	16th	Borderline
Inhibition-Inhibition	5	5th	Below Average
Inhibition-Inhibition Completion Time	8	25th	Average

Integrated Visual and Auditory (IVA+) Continuous Performance Test

The IVA+ is an EEG-validated computerized test that measures both visual and auditory impulsivity and inattention in individuals ranging in age from 6 to 96. It enables clinicians to measure and evaluate both auditory and visual inattention and impulsivity separately and simultaneously in approximately 15–20 minutes.

	Auditory Modality		Visual Modality	
Response Control	**Standard Score**	**Percentile**	**Standard Score**	**Percentile**
Prudence	85	16th	88	21st
Consistency	88	21st	80	10th
Stamina	110	76th	124	95th
Attention	**Standard Score**	**Percentile**	**Standard Score**	**Percentile**
Vigilance	66	1st	73	4th
Focus	87	18th	82	12th
Speed	123	93rd	101	54th

Wide Range Assessment of Memory and Learning, Second Edition (WRAML-2)

The WRAML-2 assesses memory and learning from multiple perspectives: visual versus verbal, rote versus meaningful. Retention is assessed in immediate, delayed recall and recognition formats.

Subtests	Immediate		Delayed		Recognition	
	Standard/ Scaled	Percentile	Standard/ Scaled	Percentile	Standard/ Scaled	Percentile
Verbal Memory	108	70th	–	–	96	39th
Story Memory	10	50th	10	50th	9	37th
Verbal Learning	13	84th	13	84th	10	50th
Visual Memory	94	34th	–	–	81	10th
Design Memory	6	9th	–	–	6	9th
Picture Memory	12	75th	–	–	8	25th
Attention/ Concentration	100	50th	–	–	–	–
Finger Windows	10	50th	–	–	–	–
Number-Letter	10	50th	–	–	–	–
General Memory	Standard = 101 Percentile = 53rd		General Recognition		Standard = 87 Percentile = 19th	

Wechsler Individual Achievement Test, Third Edition (WIAT-III)

This battery of tests measures achievement in basic academic skills and acquired information.

Composite/Subtest/ *Component*	Standard Score	Percentile Rank	Age Equivalent	Grade Equivalent
Oral Language	112	79	-	-
Listening Comprehension	115	84	7-8	2.9
Receptive Vocabulary	93	32	-	-
Oral Discourse Comprehension	130	98	-	-
Oral Expression	105	63	6-11	1.7
Expressive Vocabulary	116	86	-	-
Oral Word Fluency	102	55	-	-

Composite/Subtest/ Component	Standard Score	Percentile Rank	Age Equivalent	Grade Equivalent
Sentence Repetition	96	39	-	-
Basic Reading	96	39	-	-
Word Reading	95	37	6-0	<1.0
Pseudoword Decoding	98	45	6-0	<1.0
Oral Reading Fluency	79	8	<6-0	<1.0
Oral Reading Accuracy	82	12	<6-0	<1.0
Oral Reading Rate	73	4	<6-0	<1.0
Written Expression				
Alphabet Writing Fluency	91	27	5-4	K.5
Spelling	101	53	6-4	1.2
Mathematics	89	23	-	-
Numerical Operations	91	27	6-0	K.9
Math Problem Solving	89	23	5-8	K.8
Math Fluency	93	32	-	-
Addition	103	58	6-8	1.4
Subtraction	83	13	<6.0	<1.0

Gray Oral Reading Test, Fifth Edition (GORT-5), Form A

This assessment measures the rate, fluency and comprehension of a student's oral reading skills.

	Scaled/ Standard Score	Percentile Rank	Age Equivalent	Grade Equivalent
Oral Reading Quotient	78	7	-	-
Rate	5	5	<6.0	<1.0
Accuracy	6	9	<6.0	<1.0
Fluency (Rate + Accuracy)	5	5	<6.0	<1.0
Comprehension	7	16	<6.0	<1.0

Jordan Left-Right Reversal Test, Third Edition (Jordan-3)

This test measures a student's ability to distinguish letters, numbers, and words in their correct orientation.

	Accuracy	Error
Total Raw Score	29	23
Percentile Rank	24	1
Standard Score	**89**	**67**
Age Equivalent	5-0	-

Test of Orthographic Competence (TOC), Ages 6–7

This battery of tests measures different aspects of spelling: conventions, speed, and accuracy.

	Standard Score	Percentile Rank
Signs and Symbols	11	63
Grapheme Matching	3	1
Homophone Choice	6	9
Punctuation	11	63
Orthographic Ability	**84**	**14**

Test of Word Reading Efficiency (TOWRE), Form A

This test measures a student's ability to read sight words and nonsense words quickly and efficiently.

	Standard Score	Percentile Rank	Age Equivalent	Grade Equivalent
Sight Word Efficiency	85	16	<6.0	<1.0
Phonemic Decoding Efficiency	92	30	6.0	1.0
Total Word Reading Efficiency	88	21	-	-

About the Author

Dewey Rosetti cofounded Parents Education Network (PEN, now part of Children's Health Council), which aims to educate parents and teachers on the latest and most effective methods for helping children with learning differences succeed in school and in life. After more than 25 years of experience as an advocate for individualized learning techniques, Dewey partnered with Harvard professor and best-selling author Todd Rose to bring his revolutionary research in the "Science of Individuality" to parenting kids who learn differently.